Solving Executive Function Challenges

Solving Executive Function Challenges

Simple Ways to Get Kids with Autism Unstuck and on Target

by

Lauren Kenworthy, Ph.D.
Children's National Medical Center
Washington, D.C.

Laura Gutermuth Anthony, Ph.D.
Children's National Medical Center
Washington, D.C.

Katie C. Alexander, M.S., OTR
The Ivymount School
Rockville, Maryland

Monica Adler Werner, M.A.
The Ivymount School
Rockville, Maryland

Lynn M. Cannon, M.Ed.
The Ivymount School
Rockville, Maryland

and

Lisa Greenman, J.D.

·P A U L·H·
BROOKES
PUBLISHING CO.®

Baltimore • London • Sydney

Paul H. Brookes Publishing Co.
Post Office Box 10624
Baltimore, Maryland 21285-0624
USA

www.brookespublishing.com

Typeset by Scribe, Inc., Philadelphia, Pennsylvania.
Manufactured in the United States of America by
Versa Press, Inc., East Peoria, Illinois.

Library of Congress Cataloging-in-Publication Data
  Solving executive function challenges : simple ways to get kids with autism unstuck
and on target / Lauren Kenworthy, Ph.D. [and five others].
     pages   cm
  Summary: "An extension of Brookes's 2011 school curriculum Unstuck and On Target! An Executive Function Curriculum to Improve Flexibility for Children with Autism
Spectrum Disorders, Research Edition. Helps children with autism spectrum disorders
understand and improve flexibility by hearing the same vocabulary and encountering
the same expectations at home and school"—Provided by publisher.
  ISBN 978-1-59857-603-0 (paperback)—ISBN 1-59857-603-8 (paperback)
  1. Autism in children—Treatment. 2. Autism in children—Rehabilitation. I. Kenworthy, Lauren.

  RJ506.A9S65 2014
  618.92'85882—dc23   2013051096

British Library Cataloguing in Publication data are available from the British Library.

2023   2022   2021   2020   2019

10   9   8   7   6   5   4

Contents

About the Reproducible Materials

Print and e-book purchasers of this book may download, print, and/or photocopy Figures 3.1, 4.2, 4.3, 4.5, 5.1, 6.3, 6.5, 6.6, 6.10, and 6.11, as well as Appendix A, for educational and household use. These materials are included with the print book and are also available at **www.brookespublishing.com/kenworthy**

Clip art in select chapters, select forms, and select appendixes that appear in this book; in select downloadable forms; and in the downloadable appendix are © 2014 Jupiterimages Corporation.

About the Authors

Lauren Kenworthy, Ph.D., is the director of the Center for Autism Spectrum Disorders at Children's National Medical Center and is an associate professor of psychiatry, pediatrics, and neurology at The George Washington University Medical School. She has specialized in the neuropsychological assessment of children with social learning disorders and executive dysfunction since 1995. In addition, Dr. Kenworthy has published more than 40 peer-reviewed papers investigating autism and executive function and developed the most widely used assessment tool in the field, the Behavior Rating Inventory of Executive Function (BRIEF; with Gioia, Isquith, & Guy; Psychological Assessment Resources, 2000). She is a coauthor of *Unstuck and On Target! An Executive Function Curriculum to Improve Flexibility for Children with Autism Spectrum Disorders, Research Edition* (Paul H. Brookes Publishing Co., 2011).

Laura Gutermuth Anthony, Ph.D., is a clinical and developmental psychologist and the associate director of the Center for Autism Spectrum Disorders at Children's National Medical Center and an associate professor in the Departments of Psychiatry and Behavioral Sciences and Pediatrics at Children's National Medical Center (CNMC) in The George Washington University School of Medicine and Health Sciences. She leads the intervention program at the Center for Autism Spectrum Disorders, an interdisciplinary evaluation, treatment, research, and training clinic. Dr. Anthony has expertise in developing clinical interventions and extensive experience in studying and treating behavioral rigidities (executive dysfunction) and stereotyped behaviors in children with developmental disorders. In addition to being among the coauthors of *Unstuck and On Target! An Executive Function Curriculum to Improve Flexibility for Children with Autism Spectrum Disorders, Research Edition* (Paul H. Brookes Publishing Co., 2011), she and

Dr. Kenworthy have been Principal Investigators on two federally funded projects demonstrating the effectiveness of the Unstuck and On Target! curriculum (National Institute of Mental Health and Patient-Centered Outcomes Research Institute).

Katie C. Alexander, M.S., OTR, is an occupational therapist and served as the founding program director for the Model Asperger Program (MAP) at The Ivymount School, where she led the development and implementation of a model evidence-based educational program, including intervention addressing social competency, positive behavior supports, and executive function. She has specialized in serving individuals with autism spectrum disorder (ASD), their families, and the professionals who support them since 2000. Ms. Alexander has conducted research on cognitive behavioral intervention for adolescents with ASD and has provided trainings and presentations both nationally and at the state level. She was a coauthor of *Unstuck and On Target! An Executive Function Curriculum to Improve Flexibility for Children with Autism Spectrum Disorders, Research Edition* (Paul H. Brookes Publishing Co., 2011). Ms. Alexander continues to develop programming for individuals with ASD and to participate in the research collaboration between The Ivymount School and Children's National Medical Center.

Monica Adler Werner, M.A., is the director of the Model Asperger Program (MAP) at The Ivymount School. In that capacity, she has spearheaded the development of a social learning curriculum that emphasizes problem solving, self-advocacy, and self-regulation. Ms. Werner has been a major contributor to the development of the Unstuck and On Target! intervention and was among the coauthors of *Unstuck and On Target! An Executive Function Curriculum to Improve Flexibility for Children with Autism Spectrum Disorders, Research Edition* (Paul H. Brookes Publishing Co., 2011). In addition, she is a cofounder of Take2 Summer Camp, a program designed to develop social thinking and problem-solving skills.

Lynn Cannon, M.Ed., is the social learning coordinator at The Ivymount School. She is responsible for helping to develop and oversee the social learning and academic curriculum for the lower, middle, and high school students at The Ivymount School. Ms. Cannon is the director of Take2 Summer Camp, a program designed to develop interaction skills and social thinking in children ages 8–12. Prior to her current role at The Ivymount School, Ms. Cannon was a classroom teacher in the Model Asperger Program at Ivymount and at the Lab School of Washington, in Washington, D.C. She has been a major contributor to the development of the Unstuck and On Target! intervention and was among the coauthors of *Unstuck and On Target! An Executive Function Curriculum to Improve Flexibility for Children with Autism Spectrum Disorders, Research Edition* (Paul H. Brookes Publishing Co., 2011). Ms. Cannon has supported the data collection process, the implementation of the intervention, and the training of the teachers in the pilot feasibility and development trial.

Lisa Greenman, J.D., is an attorney in Washington, D.C., specializing in issues relating to developmental disability and mental illness that arise in the defense of death penalty cases. She is closely involved with two innovative educational programs that serve children with autism spectrum disorder, Take2 Summer Camp, which she cofounded, and The Ivymount School, where she is on the board of directors. She is also a member of the Advisory Council of the National Institute of Mental Health. Ms. Greenman is the parent of two children, one of whom has autism. She is overwhelmingly grateful for the wisdom and guidance of the coauthors of this book, from whom she and her family have learned so much.

Foreword

Recent research has revealed that 50% of children and youth with autism spectrum disorders (ASDs) experience aggressive behavior that is primarily reactive in nature (Farmer et al., 2014; Mazurek, Kanne, & Wodka, 2013). The behavior is not planned and, in my opinion, it occurs because learners with ASD do not have adequate tools to address the everyday challenges that most of us face. One of these tools is executive function (EF).

Few people truly appreciate the role of EF in daily life, and even fewer understand how to address this complex set of skills. As a result, individuals with ASD do not learn the skills they need to navigate unpredictable events, make plans and adjust as necessary, compromise, negotiate, exhibit flexibility of thought and action, and remain calm. Kenworthy, Anthony, Alexander, Werner, Cannon, and Greenman, in their marvelous book *Solving Executive Function Challenges: Simple Ways to Get Kids with Autism Unstuck and on Target* are changing this trajectory. These authors have created a manual that explains EF, describes the impact on the learner and those in his or her environments, and provides evidence-based strategies to teach EF skills in an extremely user-friendly manner.

This book fills a void that has long existed—a void that has prevented learners with ASD from reaching their potential. It is well written, uncomplicated in its presentation, and easy to implement. Furthermore, this manual is compatible with the 21st Century Student Outcomes and Support Systems (Partnership for 21st Century Skills, n.d.) that contains the common core requirements.

Finally, this book goes *beyond* autism. It can help every learner who has difficulty with the many facets of EF. It readily fits into daily instruction.

This foreword is deliberately brief, as I believe that readers need to get to the essential content of the book immediately. I can't wait to use this book. It is simple, elegant, well written, and meaningful. It has the potential to a make significant difference in the lives of children and youth with ASD and related disabilities. I am grateful that the authors of this book understand ASD and the skills needed for life success! Thank you.

Brenda Smith Myles, Ph.D.
Consultant
Ziggurat Group
Ohio Center for Autism and Low Incidence

REFERENCES

Farmer, C., Butter, E., Mazurek, M.O., Cowan, C., Lainhart, J., Cook, E.H., . . . Aman, M. (2014). Aggression in children with autism spectrum disorders and a clinic-referred group. *Autism,* DOI: 10.1177/1362361313518995.

Mazurek, M.O., Kanne, S.M., & Wodka, E.L. (2013). Physical aggression in children and adolescents with autism spectrum disorders. *Research in Autism Spectrum Disorders, 7*(3), 455–465.

Partnership for 21st Century Skills. (n.d.). *Framework for 21st century learning.* Washington, DC: Authors.

Acknowledgments

We thank the many parents, teachers, therapists, and people with autism spectrum disorder (ASD) who have taught us over the years how to help children with ASD be more flexible and goal directed. In particular we thank members of the Parent Advisory Committee to the Children's National Center for Autism Spectrum Disorders who gave us direct guidance regarding this book, including Kelly Register-Brown, Karen Gorman, and Stephen Jones.

We acknowledge the work of Mark Ylvisaker and Tim Feeny, who developed several of the scripts that are used in this intervention, such as Big Deal/Little Deal and Choice/No Choice. Their work with children who have suffered brain injuries inspired our attempts to help children with ASD learn executive functions through the use of self-regulatory scripts.

Introduction and How to Use This Manual

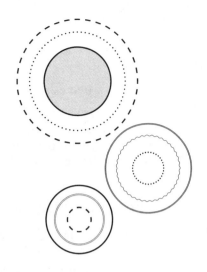

There is limited information available to parents, educators, and therapists regarding executive function (EF) in children with high-functioning autism spectrum disorder (ASD). The purpose of this guide is to support your work by giving you access to specific tools to improve EF and make life, school, and therapy easier for everyone working with a child with ASD. This manual was developed as a collaboration among researchers, teachers, therapists, and parents, including coauthor Lisa Greenman, whose son has ASD. We wanted to make an easy-to-use, practical guide that does some of the legwork for you. One parent collaborator said, "I think I already knew a lot of this stuff, but you showed me how to put it together and use it when I'm having a tough time getting my son to school in the morning!" Another said, "The information in this book is unique; you can't find it anywhere else."

WHY EXECUTIVE FUNCTION?

Executive function (EF) refers to the group of brain-based abilities everyone needs to put together information in order to act effectively and achieve goals. We have focused on EF to help a child with autism spectrum disorder (ASD) acquire the following skills:

1. Become a more flexible, independent, and successful problem solver.
2. Develop tools to self-regulate and self-advocate in more productive and socially expected ways.

- -

3.   Use a framework for solving difficult situations.

The title of this book's companion curriculum, *Unstuck and On Target!*, captures essential components of EF that are most typically impaired in ASD: Unstuck (flexibility) and On Target (organization/planning). Chapter 1 tells you more about EF in ASD.

- -

FOR WHOM IS THIS BOOK WRITTEN?

We wrote this book to support parents, teachers, therapists, and others working with elementary and early middle school children on the autism spectrum with EF challenges. We had in mind a child who spends at least some time in inclusive settings and who, ideally, is also participating in the Unstuck and On Target! program in his or her school or in a therapy setting. Unstuck and On Target! has been studied and proven effective for children whose language and intellectual abilities are at least at a third-grade level. Those children were able to answer questions, follow directions, engage in a dialogue to problem-solve, and make choices. However, we believe that these strategies will help any child and family dealing with EF challenges if the child can use language—written or oral—to engage in problem-solving. We are told that children with more limited language need modifications to simplify the language and concepts, but the reliance on visuals and simple words in this program make it accessible to them.

HOW TO USE THIS MANUAL

Research consistently supports the idea that what parents and teachers do in real-world settings such as home and school has a lasting impact on children. Research also supports using consistent strategies and tools across all the settings in which a child participates—home, school, community—to make lasting, positive, and meaningful changes in a child's life. The goal of this book is to provide you with tools to directly address a child's EF challenges through daily interactions. You will find here a problem-solving formula, daily language you can use with the child, and troubleshooting ideas that are relevant for teachers, parents, therapists, and others living or working with a child with EF challenges.

In keeping with our central theme of teaching and supporting flexibility, we have made this manual flexible in its use. Table A will help you decide where in this book to start in order to meet your needs.

Chapters 3, 4, and 5 focus on new skills and vocabulary. You will find several highlighted sections in these chapters to make the information easier to learn and apply:

- A list of Key Words and Scripts (in Chapter 3) that you can post on your refrigerator or bulletin board, in your planner, on the bathroom mirror, in the faculty room, or beside your computer.

- Several other visuals to help remind you (and children, too) of strategies available in difficult moments. Keep these handy because they can give you immediate support at those times when it can be hardest to try new interventions.

- Hands-on exercises to help you practice this approach in the Putting It into Action activities within chapters. They help you implement the ideas step by step.

Table A. How to use this manual

Chapter(s)	General concept	Who should read it?
Introduction	Overview of the book	Everyone
1	Overview of executive function (EF) • Understand the child with autism spectrum disorder's (ASD) underlying challenges and how to explain them to others. • Understand EF and develop empathy for the child's struggles, develop insight into how performance difficulties occur across settings, and foster more productive interactions.	Those who want to know what EF is and how EF looks in ASD
2, 3, 4, 5	How to teach EF skills • Principles for teaching EF • Key vocabulary and scripts to use day to day • Specific examples of how to apply scripts and vocabulary in daily life • Ideas for visual supports	Those who want to learn the strategies and vocabulary for teaching flexibility and goal-directed behavior
6	Ideas for accommodations and actions to address eight common problems	Those who need *immediate help* managing problems

MAKING UNSTUCK AND ON TARGET! A WAY OF LIFE

Share this manual, or at least the vocabulary, with other adults who interact with the child, including family members, therapists, teachers, or community members. With everyone using the same concepts and vocabulary, it will be much easier for the child to apply the new skills in different settings. A therapist or "coach" can be very helpful in working on the Unstuck and On Target! strategies in a structured and neutral environment.

We hope that you find this book practical and helpful. Parents: we know that parenting can be a tough job, and as soon as you've got one problem fixed, something else may crop up. You can't be perfect all of the time, but the more you apply the strategies in this book, the easier things will go in your family, and the more your child will feel understood and supported. Teachers: Your job isn't easy, managing a classroom full of students eager to learn, all from different backgrounds and with different abilities. The strategies and ideas in this book will support your students with flexibility, organization, and planning challenges to better follow your directions, work independently, and use your feedback. If something isn't working, try to be creative and keep trying. It has been our experience that we all (parents, teachers, and therapists) benefit from a Plan A, Plan B, Plan C, and so on (more on that to come) in the service of the important goal of promoting the success and skill acquisition of a child with ASD. It has also been our experience that, with practice and persistence, the strategies presented here will become more natural and automatic, and you will notice you're living Unstuck and On Target! every day.

What Is Executive Function, How Is It Impaired in Autism Spectrum Disorder, and Two Ways to Help

The first step in improving EF is to increase your understanding of what EF is and how it can affect a person with ASD. This understanding can also increase your empathy, as these struggles can be painful (both for the person with ASD and for those who love and work with them).

WHAT IS EXECUTIVE FUNCTION?

EF is a set of brain-based abilities that help people control their behavior (e.g., stay seated at the dinner table) and reach their goals (e.g., finish something with multiple steps, such as getting ready for school). There are many different brain-based abilities that make up EF, including the following:

- Initiation (getting started on something quickly and easily)

- Inhibition (e.g., impulse control, "putting on the brakes" and thinking before acting)

- Flexibility (e.g., shifting from one activity or idea to another, accepting a different way of seeing or doing things)

- Working memory (keeping information in mind while performing a task, e.g., remembering directions someone told you while you drive to your destination)

- Organization (e.g., keeping track of materials, understanding what the main point is, seeing the big picture and knowing what is top priority at any given time)

- Planning (developing, carrying out, and modifying a plan of action, e.g., science fair project)

- Self-monitoring (tracking your performance, e.g., "How am I doing?" "Am I doing what I am supposed to be doing?")

HOW IS EXECUTIVE FUNCTION IMPAIRED IN AUTISM SPECTRUM DISORDER?

Most people with ASD say that they have significant difficulties with EF in their daily lives. Although any aspect of EF can be disrupted in children with ASD, the most common problems are inflexibility, poor planning, and disorganization.

Children with Autism Spectrum Disorder Tend to Be Inflexible

Changes in routine and unexpected events are particularly challenging for children with ASD, and it is easy for them to get stuck on certain ideas or behaviors. Once stuck, they get distracted from whatever task is required of them at that time (e.g., homework, getting ready in the morning). Children with ASD have biologically based (preprogrammed) rigidity and inflexibility, which can appear as difficulties with the following behaviors:

- Making transitions

- Tolerating changes in routines

- Adjusting to unexpected events

- Generating new ways to approach problems

- Accepting different interpretations of rules

- Coping with strong feelings

- Responding to the needs or interests of others

- Negotiating and compromising

- Accepting different viewpoints

- Changing behavior when a situation is not going well

"Asperger's is like a vise on your brain. And each unexpected event is like another turn on the vise . . . it just keeps building until you feel like you're going to explode! Sometimes when you explode, it comes out the wrong way."

—A 13-year-old with ASD describing what it feels like to "get stuck"

Most people have some trouble being flexible at times. It can be hard for anyone to adjust to some changes. For example, beginning a new job or having a first child is stressful. There are also ways that we think about things that may be hard to change. It is possible for anybody to get "stuck in a rut" of doing things in a certain way or thinking in a certain way.

> "Aspergian focus helped me become successful by allowing me to focus on my interests to the exclusion of all else. . . . Resolve is another secret to my success. I'd like to paint this in a noble light, but a lot of my resolve is probably just common pigheadedness combined with Aspergian obliviousness."
>
> —John Elder Robison in *Be Different: Adventures of a Free-Range Aspergian*[1]

Inflexibility can also be a good thing. For example, most of us have a morning routine that we more or less follow when getting ready to leave the house. This prevents us from realizing only in the car on the way to work that we forgot to brush our teeth. Inflexibility can also drive deep investigations into specific topics or areas of interest that can result in someone becoming a valued expert, like Temple Grandin, Ph.D., or John Elder Robison (see quotation above). However, when problems accepting change, making transitions, shifting thoughts, or moving on become so extreme that they interfere with everyday functioning, it is time to learn how to become more flexible.

Children with Autism Spectrum Disorder Tend to Have Poor Planning and Disorganization

The expression "can't see the forest for the trees" captures the organization style of many children with ASD. They tend to have trouble organizing things, such as their rooms, school materials, homework, and belongings. They also have trouble identifying the main idea and organizing their thinking in ways that are accessible to most others. This means that they have trouble "showing" what they know in school. They struggle to get their ideas across to others and to pull information together, synthesizing complex and different information into a cohesive whole.

This cognitive style can also be an asset. Children with ASD tend to excel at remembering details and methodically analyzing information. Their heightened awareness and attention to detail may be useful in detective work (it is no accident that Sherlock Holmes shows many signs of ASD), computer programming, math, engineering, medical pathology, and other jobs that require logical and detail-oriented approaches. However, such children often have difficulty organizing tasks that have several steps and setting or keeping track of goals and instructions that should guide their work.

When inflexibility and disorganization combine with other EF challenges common in ASD, such as problems with self-awareness and self-monitoring, it becomes very hard for children on the autism spectrum to get even basic tasks done. The following vignettes about Johnny and Suzy show what this looks like in real life.

Johnny and Suzy are smart 10-year-old twins, and their parents want them to learn how to be more independent with their morning routine. They talk through the key steps the children need to complete before going to school, and both children easily explain what the steps are and how to do them. The twins' parents are confident that both children have the required skills for this. Johnny has autism spectrum disorder. Suzy does not. Table 1.1 describes what happens when the twins try to put their knowledge into action at home.

Table 1.1. What does flexible, organized, and goal-directed planning look like at home?

Johnny	Suzy
Goes to sleep Sunday night saying he will get up at 8 a.m. and easily make his 8:30 bus. His alarm goes off at 8 a.m. He turns it off, sees his favorite book lying by the bed, starts to read, and *loses track of his goal*. He is still reading 10 minutes later when his dad comes and tells him he'll be late for school.	Makes a *plan* the night before about what she will need/do in the morning. Walks through the steps in her mind and decides that she needs 45 minutes to get everything done and would like an extra 15 minutes to read the comics, so she sets her alarm for 7:30 a.m. in order to make her 8:30 bus. The alarm goes off and she *gets started (initiates)* easily, turns it off, and gets out of bed.
Looks around his room for his favorite shirt to wear. Finds it dirty and crumpled in a corner. Is *inflexible*. Can't consider any other clothing that he could wear. Storms out of his room in his pajamas and slams the door.	*Organized* the night before: laid out the clothes she wanted to wear and put her homework and school materials in her backpack. In the morning, she gets dressed and starts down to eat breakfast, but realizes she slept on her hair wrong and it looks funny. Stops to get it wet and comb it.

Johnny's mother asks him what is wrong and helps him find a clean shirt that is acceptable to him. She asks him to come down quickly and eat breakfast, as it is getting late. Johnny goes to the bathroom, starts reading a magazine, and has *trouble starting (initiating)* the next step of the routine. Mom calls him three times with increasing irritation. Finally, he goes downstairs, doesn't *check/monitor* time, and sees his dog. He is *distracted from his goal* and plays with his dog. His father finds him and tells him his breakfast is cold and he has 5 minutes to eat, brush his teeth, and leave for the bus. Johnny decides he doesn't have time to eat breakfast, which means he will feel hungry all morning in addition to not being able to wear his favorite shirt, and he gets *stuck* and overwhelmed. Runs up to his room.

Suzy fixes her hair and remains *focused on the goal* of getting to her bus on time. Heads downstairs. Her father tells her she looks nice. *Checks/monitors* how fast she is moving through the morning routine and realizes that she is running a few minutes late. *Flexibly* adjusts by speeding up her pace. Pats dog on the head quickly when he comes by and *persists* with eating. Remains calm. Reads comics quickly. Mother notes that she is right on time and doing a great job.

Mother comes up, calms him down as best she can, gives him a Pop Tart to eat on the way to the bus, and tells him to come downstairs and get his backpack. Because he *didn't plan* ahead and set up his backpack the night before, he realizes he doesn't have his homework. He looks about frantically for it in a *disorganized* fashion in random parts of the house.

Brushes her teeth, grabs the backpack she set up the night before, gets a goodbye hug from her mother, and heads for the bus.

Father loses his temper, says Johnny will miss the bus unless he leaves right now, and tells him to forget his homework. Johnny runs out the door but misses the bus anyway. Comes home and his mother drives him to school, but she is mad because she is now late. Arrives late to school without homework.

Catches bus, goes to school. Turns in last night's homework to teacher, who praises her.

Outcome: Johnny is late and unprepared. Parents are stressed, and Johnny feels frustrated, irritable, and dependent on others.

Outcome: Suzy is on time and prepared for school. Parents are satisfied that she handles her morning routine well, and Suzy feels confident and independent.

Time elapsed: 1½ hours

Time elapsed: 1 hour

Number of parental prompts required: 13

Number of parental prompts required: 0

Ratio of negative to positive feedback: 10:1

Ratio of negative to positive feedback: 0:3

Here is an example of how Johnny and Suzy's executive function abilities affect them in a reader–writer workshop class. They are each articulate children with good spelling and grammar skills. They both generally express good ideas in class discussions and clearly have the verbal knowledge to tackle today's assignment. They are starting a new unit on biography, and the assignment is to pick a hero they want to read and write about. Table 1.2 describes what happens when they try to put their knowledge into action.

Table 1.2. What does flexible, organized, and goal-directed planning look like at school?

Johnny	Suzy
Arrives a few minutes late to his reader–writer workshop class because he is generally *disorganized* with his materials and had forgotten his notebook and had to go back and get it. He doesn't hear the teacher's full introduction to the new unit, but sees on the blackboard that the students are to select a hero to read and write about. He doesn't pay attention to the specific sequence of tasks required, write anything down about the assignment, or *plan* the steps he needs to take to complete it. He *does* decide immediately that he will read all about dolphins. He loves sea mammals and has been studying them in science. He thinks that dolphins are his heroes because they are surviving against all odds.	Is on time to class, is well *organized,* and has a notebook with a section for reader–writer workshop in which she writes down the directions as the teacher is both saying them and writing them on the board: "two-page biography, rough draft is due in 1 week, final copy in 2 weeks, topic: my hero, read three sources, not Wikipedia, list sources and use information from each of them in the biography." Suzy writes the two due dates in her agenda book as well and makes a *plan* about when she needs to complete specific parts of the assignment, deciding she will pick a topic today and identify her three sources of information, read the sources by the end of the week, and write the rough draft next Monday.
His teacher knows that he arrived late and comes to check in individually with Johnny about whether he understands the assignment and has picked a topic. Johnny says yes, although he hasn't written down any details. He says he will write about dolphins, and is *inflexible* when his teacher says that the hero has to be a human being. He argues with the teacher *impulsively* about his right to decide who will be his hero. His teacher spends 5 minutes helping Johnny calm down and, with her help, Johnny agrees to pick Jacques Cousteau, a famous sea explorer who had a special fondness for sea mammals.	*Initiates (gets started)* on the project easily and thinks about who she could pick for her hero. She considers several options and *flexibly* considers each in terms of how easy it will be to get information on the person and also how interesting the person is to her. She picks Marie Curie.

Without a *plan* for completing the assignment and still *stuck* on dolphins, Johnny heads straight for the teacher's tiny classroom library, which has a book on dolphins he has been wanting to look at. He knows he needs to investigate Cousteau, but figures that there might be something in this book about him. As he reads the book, however, he is quickly *distracted from the goal* of writing a biography and enjoys the pictures of dolphins. He is surprised when the teacher says reader–writer workshop is over and is upset because he hasn't finished the book. The teacher sees his distress and again comes to his desk and works out a plan with him whereby he can take the book home overnight to finish it. She also tells him that for homework, he needs to research Cousteau on the Internet to find three sources about him that he can use for his biography. Johnny says okay.

Checks/monitors time and sees that she has 20 minutes left in the class period. Asks teacher if she can go to the library to search for sources. Gets permission, and uses time in library effectively because she remains *focused on her goal* of finding three books on Marie Curie. Returns to class with three books as reader–writer workshop is ending.

Arrives at reader–writer workshop the next day not having done the homework. Is *distracted,* and starts chatting with a tablemate about dolphins until the teacher checks in with him again and asks if he has found three sources on Cousteau yet. He says no, he forgot, and she asks a parent volunteer to walk him to the library and help him find three books on Cousteau. He finds the books and, with the volunteer's help, starts to take notes on one of them. However, he writes down irrelevant details and has trouble separating details from the main point. He loses sight of the *goal* and gets distracted again by the dolphin photos in the books. He also hates to write and writes down very little. The next day, he forgets the books at home. He gets upset and is *stuck* on the idea that he can only read the three books at home. The teacher sits down with him to suggest getting one other book to read that day in class. The teacher e-mails Johnny's parents and asks them to help him work on the project over the weekend.

Arrives at reader–writer workshop the next day with the three books she has checked out and continues to follow her *plan*. She reads through one of the books and takes notes. Reader–writer workshop comes to an end, and she *checks/monitors* how far she has gotten in the assignment and realizes that tomorrow she will have to complete notes on the other two books, which she does.

(continued)

Table 1.2.   (*continued*)

Johnny	Suzy
On Monday, Johnny comes in with some notes he has dictated to his mother, and his teacher gives him a second copy of the writing prompts for writing the biography. He becomes *inflexible* about the fact that he doesn't think the writing prompts are good. The teacher must pull him aside again, and asks him to "just write about anything you want about Jacques Cousteau." Johnny writes a four-sentence paragraph with short sentences: "Jacques Cousteau loved sea mammals. Dolphins are my favorite sea mammal. They are more intelligent than people. They are endangered by global warming."	On Monday, Suzy brings her notes to reader–writer workshop, using both her agenda and her good *working memory* skills to keep track of the fact that today she will work on her rough draft. She writes a well-*organized* rough draft using the prompts the teacher has provided, and gives it to the teacher to review.
The next day, Johnny refuses to make any edits based on the teacher's comments on his rough draft. At this point, his teacher decides to try a new strategy and lets him dictate to a classroom volunteer. He produces much more information this way, but is it still *poorly organized* and does not follow the rubric.	Suzy *flexibly* incorporates the teacher's edits and turns in a final version of her biography that includes all components described in the assignment rubric.
Outcome: Johnny did little reading, learned no new material, and did not respond to the writing prompt. His writing was below grade level when compared to his placement and his apparent intelligence and verbal abilities. His teacher is concerned by his "lack of effort" and motivation to succeed in her class.	Outcome: Suzy got an opportunity to explore a new hero in her area of interest, science. She learned about Marie Curie's early life in the books she selected, gained research skills, and practiced her free writing and revising skills. She also enhanced her reputation with her teacher, who sees her as an intelligent, hard-working student.
Amount of 1:1 teacher time required: 60 minutes	Amount of 1:1 teacher time required: 10 minutes

These observations are supported by scientific research that documents generally poor EF in children with ASD.[2–5] Research clearly links problems with flexibility and organization/planning in ASD to differences in brain structure and function, showing that brain biology, not willfulness or laziness, drives EF differences in ASD.[6,7]

Although there are strengths that come with EF difficulties, there are also major costs. Being smart is not enough to guarantee success in the world. You have probably felt frustrated at times when your child, client, or student seemed unable to use, or act on, his or her excellent knowledge base. Intervention to improve flexibility and goal-directed behavior, along with good social skills training, can help a child with ASD be more successful and independent in school, social, and work settings. There are many important books on teaching social skills to children with ASD. The focus of this book is on how to improve the child's EF skills so that he or she can stay flexible and unstuck and use on-task, goal-directed behaviors to stay on target and successfully navigate each day. These are essential skills for lifelong success.

TWO WAYS TO HELP: CHANGE THE ENVIRONMENT AND TEACH NEW SKILLS

All people who spend much time with children know that it is important to "pick your battles." Building on that wisdom, there are two approaches you can take to support a child in difficult situations. The first approach is to *change the environment*. You probably do this all the time. You find quiet rooms, cut tags out of clothing, or carry headphones, snacks, preferred books, or toys when going new places. This is called *accommodation*.

The second approach is to *teach new skills*. You want the best possible outcome for the child with ASD. That requires you to manage, and eventually teach the child to manage, a complex balancing act between his or her biologically inflexible, detail-focused brain and a world that requires almost continuous flexibility and integration of information (because of ever-changing settings, task demands, and other factors). Managing this balancing act using new skills is called *remediation*.

Working carefully on changing the environment as you are teaching new flexibility and organizational skills will improve the child's ability to cope with all situations. It will also provide a model the child can learn from. He or she will eventually need to develop the self-awareness and self-advocacy skills to determine when it is appropriate to be flexible versus when to ask for flexibility from the environment. Finally, the two-pronged approach validates your child's experience of how hard it is to be flexible.

- -

Change the Environment

"An ounce of prevention is worth a pound of cure."

—Benjamin Franklin

Communication and the integration and organization of information are challenging for people with ASD, who can be easily overwhelmed in social, group, and new situations. Once overwhelmed, any child may feel more anxious, behave more impulsively, and show more unusual types of behavior. Unusual and impulsive behaviors put a child at risk for being teased and bullied or socially isolated. Sometimes, being inflexible in a situation that might otherwise be overwhelming can help a child to limit the number of unexpected events to which he or she must respond, reduce anxiety, and increase his or her ability to behave appropriately.

Think about it this way: if your child had a reading disability, would you expect him or her to read all day long? No! You would provide breaks and downtime when your child could recharge and get ready to try again. Children with ASD have social and executive disabilities that affect them in all environments, not just on a specific task like reading. Sometimes they need a break during which they are not required to be flexible or make sense of complex and confusing situations. As Ari Ne'eman, president of the Autism Self-Advocacy Network said,

> Don't forget that social situations can be like a minefield for those of us with autism. In a minefield, you would be very cautious and resistant to making any sudden, unplanned moves. Likewise, inflexibility provides order in the context of a world that is confusing and illogical for us. (Personal communication, February 3, 2010)

As a parent or teacher, you are a key person to advocate for and implement accommodations (e.g., predictable, posted schedules) that will increase the child's sense of security and ability to learn. You may also need to help the child avoid specific intolerable situations or tasks that are too risky for him or her. For example, it is sometimes better for the child not to eat lunch in a large, crowded, overwhelming cafeteria, but instead to eat in a classroom. Intolerable situations or tasks may require so much effort or energy that a child becomes exhausted and can't do further work. Such situations may overwhelm him or her and create high risk for impulsive, interfering behaviors, or they may make him or her too anxious. These are situations that the child needs to learn how to recognize and avoid. Avoiding an overloading environment is not a failure, but rather a success of self-awareness and self-advocacy. In fact, every successful person learns to seek out environments and situations that set him or her up for success and to avoid those are a set-up for failure. Chapter 6 provides troubleshooting on potential problems and will give you lots of ideas about how to modify or avoid difficult situations or tasks for children with ASD.

Teach New Skills

"Give a man a fish, feed him for a day.
Teach a man to fish, feed him for a lifetime."

—Lao Tzu

A big part of improving the match between an inflexible, detail-oriented brain and inclusive environments (e.g., regular education and work settings) is to explicitly teach the person with ASD how to become more flexible, organized, and goal oriented. You will learn how to do this in the next chapters of this book. Embedded in these chapters are various ideas that often include both accommodation and remediation, and you will have the most success if you maintain a careful balance of each as you try to implement the strategies in the following chapters.

Overview of the Unstuck and on Target! Intervention

The Unstuck and On Target! program teaches three EF skills using four key teaching methods.

THREE EXECUTIVE FUNCTION SKILLS

Through the Unstuck and On Target! program, children learn

1. *Flexibility,* or how to handle unexpected events and unwanted demands more easily

2. *Goal setting,* or how to see the "big picture," make long-term goals, and avoid distractions along the way

3. *Making and checking plans,* or how to organize the steps necessary to accomplish a goal or a task and monitor their work

How do these skills make a child more successful? Most parents and teachers take the long view of what it means for a child to be successful. As such, our primary goal is that our children or students become happy, well-functioning adults who are employed and have satisfying relationships with others. The three skills are fundamental for finding success in one's community and for identifying and pursuing dreams. School curricula usually target short-term academic or behavioral goals because they are written for one specific school year, which partially explains why EF skills are not often addressed in school. However, students need these skills to manage time and studying and to develop positive relationships with their peers.

How does teaching children these skills make your life easier? As parents, therapists, and teachers ourselves, we know that these are all demanding jobs and that, to be as effective as you can be and still have fun, it is important to find tricks and teach children skills that will make your job easier. The more EFs children can do independently, the less you have to do for them. We are used to following toddlers around and making decisions and carrying out routines for them, but once a child is school age or older, it is exhausting to continue operating as their EF system 24/7. Teaching the child the three skills of flexibility, goal setting, and planning will make your job a little simpler (Figure 2.1). The advantage of the Unstuck and on Target! program is that it embeds executive strategies, thereby not adding more load but rather reallocating time from frustrating and unproductive interactions to teaching efficient strategies.

HOW DO YOU MAKE IT HAPPEN? FOUR TEACHING METHODS

The following subsections describe four methods for teaching EF skills that work well for children with ASD. In the future, when you want a child with ASD to learn any new skill, whether or not it relates to EF, you can use these same techniques (summarized in Figure 2.2).

Memorize and Repeatedly Use Scripts and Key Words

Children with ASD, even those with large vocabularies, are easily overwhelmed by spoken directions and reminders. They can also be inflexible about the meaning of words. Using streamlined, highly consistent language (i.e., key words that you always use the same way) helps them process your message more easily. In fact, you could say that consistency is ASD's Golden Rule. So,

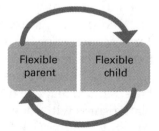

Figure 2.1. Flexibility in a parent promotes flexibility in a child, and vice versa.

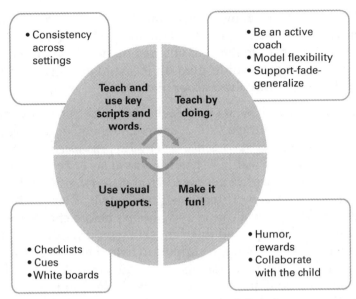

Figure 2.2.   Four teaching methods of Unstuck and On Target!

for each EF skill, parents, teachers, and therapists need to use the same phrases (or scripts) and words over and over for consistency between home, school, and therapies. Examples of Unstuck and On Target! scripts and vocabulary include "Is this a big deal or a little deal?" "What is your goal?" "Compromise," and "Let's make a Plan B." The more people in a child's life who understand and use these scripts and key words, and the more they are used in as many places and situations as possible, the more proficient the child will become at generalizing them to new people, places, and situations.

Teach by Doing: Model and Coach to Teach New Scripts and Skills

Teaching EF skills and habits is like teaching a musical instrument or a sport. You can provide information about how to kick a ball or play a melody, but most of the teaching comes when you model the skill (show them how it is done) and guide them as they practice it. This book shows you how to model flexibility and then help children practice flexibility in real-life situations. A few key principles will guide you:

- Just as when learning an instrument or a sport, *expect children to need to practice the same skills repeatedly.* Don't give up if they can't demonstrate the skill you just modeled, any more than a music teacher would give up if a student didn't play the scale just the way the teacher played it.

- You are a coach who encourages the child to get closer and closer to mastering a skill over time. Remember to start with the basics. *Most successful teaching happens when you teach a child a new skill that is just barely beyond his or her current skill set.* That is why most people teach children to ride a bike with training wheels first. Teachers do this daily; they teach addition before multiplication and phonics before chapter books. Once you have picked the right skill, you provide modeling, cueing, and just enough support to help the child be successful. When you first start using the EF scripts, you will use them to talk about yourself. For example, you might model goal setting by saying, "I'd really like to skip cooking tonight and go out for dinner, but my bigger goal is to save up money for our family trip, so I'm going to choose to skip the restaurant and save my money."

- You will need to *provide just enough coaching and support for the child to demonstrate the new skill, and be ready to reduce, or fade, your coaching slowly as he or she masters it.* You are already an expert at this. For example, parents, you taught your child how to dress himself or herself not by saying one day, "Get dressed," but rather by showing him or her what to do step by step, and reducing your support when you saw that your child had mastered the steps in the process. To promote better EF and generalization of the skills, a common pattern of gradually fading supports (see Figure 2.3) would occur as follows:

  1. Teach a new script (in the chapters that follow, we give you examples of how to do this).

Figure 2.3. Gradually fading support.

2. Fade the full script to a few key words (e.g., "What's your plan?" "Choice or no choice?").

3. Later on, when the child needs even less direction, you may decrease your coaching and just offer a simple gesture or a meaningful glance, and that will prompt him or her to use the script in new situations (generalization).

- *Remember to watch and ask questions before you jump in with guidance.* Sometimes you need to watch children and ask them leading questions (e.g., "What do you need to do next?") in order to figure out what they already can do and to know when to back off. Unless you are planning to attend college or go to work with him or her, your long-term goal is for the child to be able to use the skills taught in this book independently. It may take several years, but if you slowly fade or limit your support, new skills will grow and develop.

- *Remember to have patience with yourself and the child as you move through this process.* The key to learning is repetition, and children will get things wrong, even after it seems they know it. Learning these skills takes time and repetition. That's why it's important to start teaching them early and giving lots of different kinds of opportunities to practice. For example, children may "know" their seven times tables, but forget 7 times 8 during a mad-minute quiz. They may need to go back and review their math facts again to get to fluency.

Make It Fun: We All Learn Better and Teach Better When We Are Having Fun

There is lots of evidence that people learn best from positive experiences and praise as opposed to reprimands and corrections.[8] Following are suggestions for how to keep the interaction positive with a child, even when teaching difficult new skills like flexibility and goal setting.

- *One key to having fun is developing a collaboration with the child.* Seek his or her input about how to solve problems, what gets in the way, and what would help. Assist in setting goals and developing vocabulary (e.g., "This is a Gumby moment; I need to be extra flexible."). When teaching new skills, it is essential to target everyday problems with which children want help and to provide tricks to help them reach goals they care about. If a child doesn't want to fix a major problem, then the first step is to work on motivation, which can include helping the child understand how the problem will get in the way of goals or will prevent him or her from obtaining things that he or she does want. For example, lots of children want more control over their choices but might need help realizing that learning to be flexible will actually give them more control or freedom in the end. The more "say" a child has in what skills or goals to work on and which tricks to use (e.g., paper checklist versus a visual diagram, what the rewards will be, what coping skills are most helpful), the more likely he or she will be to use them.

- *Both you and the child will work harder on flexibility routines if they make you laugh or feel good.* We have provided tips in later chapters on how to have fun when teaching each of the EF skills that we hope will inspire your own creative and playful instincts. For example, to teach goal setting, you might set a goal of determining the best-tasting ice cream at the local ice cream shop. You will also get a lot more mileage out of praising flexible behavior and showing how being flexible gets the child more of what he or she wants, including more independence and privileges, than you will by criticizing.

- *Figure out how laugh at your failures.* Everyone will feel better if the stakes are lower. If you need inspiration for this idea, watch the TV show Mythbusters and quote their assertion, "Failure is always an option." Stories about plans that didn't work out can become "inside jokes" among parents, therapists, teachers, and children. Talking about an "epic fail" of a plan you masterminded helps create a strong relationship, models how to handle failure, and sets the stage for how you will respond to failed plans. In addition, laughing together over a failed plan, or destroying a failed plan together can be fun (teachers we know have shredded plans, burned plans— outside of course—and stomped on bad plans), and then should be followed by doing something fun together such as playing a game. The memory of the outrageous destruction of the bad plan becomes a model for what we do to bad plans and how to recover to make yet another plan.

Provide Visual Supports

We all learn new habits more easily when we have concrete reminders of what we need to do (this is why sticky notes work so well!). This is especially true for people with ASD. You will find it helpful to post visuals, such as the list of key flexibility vocabulary words and scripts provided with this manual, on your refrigerator, bulletin board, computer, or in other prominent places. Each of the coming chapters ends with ideas for, and specific examples of, visual cues to keep everyone unstuck and on target. You can copy these materials right out of this book or change them if you want to. Chapter 6 (Troubleshooting) offers some additional ideas for visuals. Either way, be sure to share the ones you use with everyone working with the child, so parents, therapists, and teachers are all on the same page!

Unstuck

*Teaching a
Child to Be Flexible*

This chapter will cover the steps you will take to teach flexible thinking and behavior. Particularly important are the scripts and vocabulary words: try to use them daily!

WHAT IS COGNITIVE FLEXIBILITY, AND WHY IS BEING FLEXIBLE IMPORTANT?

Physical flexibility allows people to bend without breaking, fit into small places, and get dressed in the morning. *Cognitive* flexibility is what allows people to generate more than one solution or answer, recognize when a strategy or response is not working and develop a new approach, consider complex or conflicting information (e.g., Hamlet is a hero, but he also makes mistakes), and negotiate or compromise. For many people on the autism spectrum, cognitive inflexibility (or rigidity) gets in the way of making friends, learning in an inclusive classroom, or holding down a job. Increasing a child's cognitive flexibility makes parents', teachers', and therapists' lives easier, too. It reduces the amount of time you must spend negotiating over nonnegotiables (e.g., the child has to attend school) and intervening to help the child move on from an insult from a sibling or peer or adjust to an unavoidable change in plans. The Flexibility, Stuck, Plan A/Plan B, Compromise, Big Deal/Little Deal, and Choice/No Choice[9,10] scripts taught in this chapter give you quick phrases that will help a child switch gears more easily and efficiently.

KEY FLEXIBILITY WORDS AND PHRASES

Flexibility

Stuck

Plan A/Plan B

Compromise

Big Deal/Little Deal

Choice/No Choice

Flexible Is Strong!

See Figure 3.1, Unstuck and On Target! Key Words and Scripts chart, for a version of this list you can post.

WHAT ARE THE KEY WORDS AND SCRIPTS OR PHRASES?

Flexible: Being flexible means we can change our ideas, do something different from what we thought we would do, think about something differently, consider new information, and keep an open mind. When we are flexible we have many choices. Use phrases such as the following:

- "I need to be flexible."

- "How can we be flexible in this situation?"

- "Let's think of a way we can be flexible in case our first plan doesn't work out."

- "Being flexible helps me get some of what I want."

- "I can't always get what I want, so I need to be flexible."

- "Being flexible feels better than being stuck."

- "I can be flexible; I've done it before."

- "It's okay, we'll find another way."

- "When you did X, I could tell that you were being flexible, and it worked!"

- "Thank you for being flexible with Y, it made things much easier."

Unstuck and On Target!
Key Words and Scripts

Flexible
- If I am flexible, more good things happen to me.
- I love how you were flexible: flexible is strong!

Unstuck
- I'm getting stuck on _____. How can I get unstuck?
- Since you got unstuck, now we have more choices.

Compromise
- Let's compromise so we both get some of what we want.
- Great job compromising!

On Target
- What is our target goal? Is this a whim?
- Are we on target right now?

Plan A/ Plan B
- What is our Plan B?
- You always think of great plans.

Big Deal/ Little Deal
- How can we turn this big deal into a little deal?
- I know that was a big deal. Great job turning it into a little deal.

Choice/ No Choice
- Do we have a choice about that? Is this a no-choice situation?
- High fives for handling that no-choice situation so well!

Goal	Plan	Do	Check
What do we want to do?	How will we do it?	Let's try our plan.	How did it work?

Figure 3.1. Unstuck and On Target! Key Words and Scripts.

Stuck and Unstuck: When you are stuck, you only have one choice: to be stuck. There's nothing that you can do when you are stuck. Doing the same thing over and over again is unlikely to get you out of the situation and it is likely to make you feel increasingly bad. Think of the last time your car got stuck in the snow or mud. Pressing on the gas harder only got you more stuck. You have to do something different to get unstuck. Use phrases such as the following:

- "I'm stuck, what can I do?"

- "Are you stuck?"

- "How can I get unstuck?"

- "I'm stuck in the mud" (which provides a visual image of why being stuck is unpleasant).

- "Being stuck feels awful."

- "When I am stuck I only have one option—to be stuck. That is no fun!"

- "I'm getting nervous, and my stomach feels tight. I can tell that I'm getting stuck. I need to think of a way to get unstuck."

- "Your face and your voice tell me that you're feeling stuck (be as specific as you can with what you know of the child's outward signs of being stuck). I want to help. Let's think of something we can do to help you get unstuck."

- "I could tell that you were getting stuck because of (provide specific example), and I saw when you got unstuck. Great job!"

Plan A/Plan B: We all have a way that we would like things to go; we call that Plan A. Plan A will not always work out, so we will need a Plan B. Plan A/Plan B is used to communicate that it is normal, and even expected, that things don't go exactly as we plan, and that sometimes it is important to switch plans or come up with a Plan B. Plan A/Plan B helps people understand that it is not their fault when something goes wrong or does not go the way they expected. Having a Plan B allows you to keep an open mind, maintain choices, avoid getting stuck, and accomplish your goals. Use phrases such as the following:

- "What's your Plan A? Do you have a Plan B, so we can make sure we accomplish our goal?"

- "What's our Plan B? Should we come up with a Plan C just in case?"

- "My Plan A isn't working. I need a Plan B."

- "Having a Plan B makes me feel better, because I know I can still accomplish my goal."

- "I need a Plan B so I don't get stuck."

- "With a Plan B, I have a good backup plan if Plan A doesn't happen."

- "You used your Plan B! That's terrific being flexible!"

- "I'm so glad that we had a Plan B. We could have gotten really stuck."

- "I love that you have a Plan A and a Plan B. That's great planning."

Compromise: In contrast to "giving in," which means that you do not get anything that you want, compromise means that two people each give up part of what they want or are flexible about the order in which they get what they want. It is important when using this word with a child that you make sure that you are proposing a true compromise in which you both get part of what you want. Use phrases such as the following:

- "Let's compromise. You go first, but then it will be my turn."

- "We can compromise so we both get some of what we want."

- "What's a good compromise?"

- "Thank you for compromising with your friend. You both got part of what you wanted and were able to keep having a good time."

- "Thank you for compromising with me. You got a little of what you wanted, and I got a little of what I wanted."

Big Deal/Little Deal: Not every hiccup in life is a big deal, but for children with ASDs little events can be experienced as very serious and feel very upsetting. Helping children learn to distinguish the difference between situations that cannot be ignored (the "big deals") as opposed to situations that are just mildly annoying (the "little deals") can help them cope and make better decisions. Acknowledging that a child thinks that something is a "big deal" and helping him or her to figure out how to address it and make it into a "little deal" is even more important. Don't tell the child that something is a little deal; instead, ask the following questions or use the following phrases:

- "Does this feel like a big deal or a little deal?"

- "How can we turn this big deal into a little deal?" If this is hard for the child to answer, say, "Let's see if we can make this a little deal by. . . ."

- "This feels like a big deal to me; can you help me make it a little deal?"

- "This is a really big deal, and I can tell that it's so big that it's creating really big feelings. Let's do (indicate calming activity)." Once child is calmer, say, "I can see this is a big deal, but I can also see a solution to make it a bit smaller. Are you ready to hear it?"

- "I could tell that felt like a big deal to you, but you stayed calm and worked with me to make it a little deal. You're such a terrific problem solver!"

- "Great job turning a big deal into a little deal."

- "Let's be problem shrinkers and turn this big deal into a little deal."

   Choice/No Choice: Often we have choices. There are usually different ways to solve a problem: we can often select among different options on a menu or at a movie theater and we can often choose when we will do something. There are other situations in which there is no choice. We have to pay taxes, go to school, go to the doctor, and leave the building when the fire alarm rings. It is important for children with ASD to learn the difference between choice and no-choice situations. It helps them understand when they can try to persuade others as opposed to when they have to flexibly accommodate a no-choice situation. It also makes clear to them that no-choice situations are not the result of you or someone else choosing to force them to do something; they are just the way the world works. It can be helpful for a child to explicitly learn that there are some situations in which, as much as he or she doesn't like it, there is no choice. Spending time and energy trying to make a choice when there is no choice will just waste time when he or she could be doing something fun, or will result in the loss of privileges to do things he or she likes. For this script to be successful, you have to emphasize choice over no-choice situations. Go out of your way to identify choice situations, and reserve "no choice" only for truly no-choice situations. Key phrases are the following:

- "I don't want to do this, but it is a no-choice situation, so I'll do it and get it over with."

- "Is this a choice or no-choice situation?"

- "Do I have a choice or do I have no choice?"

- "You have a choice here."

- "This is a no-choice instance because. . . ."

- "This is a choice situation."

- "Thank you for staying calm even when there were no choices."

- "What choice will you make?"

- "There will be a no-choice situation today (explain the no-choice situation). Let's make a plan for how we will face our no-choice situation."

- "I don't have any other choice, so I must do this. I'll take a deep breath and then do it one step at a time. I've done this before, and I know I can do it again."

Flexible Is Strong: It is difficult for people with ASD to be flexible. Like most of us, people with ASD can't do something that is hard without understanding how it will benefit them. The reasons for being flexible are not intuitive for people with ASD. So you have to explicitly teach them the answers to the questions, "Why be flexible?" and "What's in it for me?"

Help the child understand that being flexible has advantages. Show him or her that a rubber band is stronger than uncooked spaghetti because it is flexible. Point out that you can sit down when you are tired because your body is flexible. Demonstrate that we can't always get everything we want no matter how hard we try, so being flexible lets us get some of what we want. Show that being flexible helps a person to be a good friend. If we want to keep friends, we have to be flexible sometimes. You can even demonstrate that being flexible with parents or teachers helps make them happy and more likely to give the child the privileges and freedom that he or she wants. The message you are communicating is that in the end, flexibility puts the child in control and feeling strong. Here are scripts that help many children with ASD remember why they work on flexibility:

- "I can't always get everything I want. Being flexible helps me get something I want."

- "When I am flexible I get part (of what I want) and feel good in my heart."

- "It's okay; I'll find another way."

- "Flexible is strong!"

TIP
Feeling Overwhelmed by This New Vocabulary?

- *Don't let the perfect be the enemy of the good.* We know that it is impossible to say just the right thing every time or even most of the time. Shoot for optimal, not perfect. You are doing well if you use some of this vocabulary some of the time.

- *Choose 1:* Select one of the scripts to integrate into all your interactions with a child. If you try to integrate all of them at once, it will feel overwhelming to you and the child. Once you feel comfortable with the first script, integrate others (Flexible → Stuck → Plan A → Plan B).

- *Remember that you are probably already using some of these flexibility words and scripts naturally—you just aren't saying them out loud.* You already have a lot of these skills. If you can learn to be explicit and narrate what you are doing—even some of the time—you will help the child with autism spectrum disorder learn to be more flexible.

- -

TEACH BY DOING: HOW TO MODEL BEING FLEXIBLE/UNSTUCK

We all experience moments in our day when we need to be flexible. By demonstrating and explaining your own flexibility in these situations, including your emotions and decisions, you can provide children with clear examples of how they can be in control and flexible. Say out loud what you are thinking and doing, making each step obvious. Be sure to explicitly note what advantages you get from being flexible. Over time, allow the child to help you talk through the process. Most children become especially engaged with this if you ask them to help you solve your problem. The key is to use consistent language, based on the vocabulary and scripts presented in this chapter. Be creative in looking for natural opportunities to model flexibility. We have learned a lot from parents, teachers, and therapists of children with ASD over the years about how to use these golden moments to teach, and we share some examples with you in the bulleted list that follows. See also Putting It into Action: Making Flexibility Scripts a Habit at the end of this chapter.

- *At breakfast:* You could say, "There is no milk for my cereal this morning and I am getting stuck. I guess it's time for me to come up with a Plan B and make toast for breakfast. It's not what I wanted the most, but I will get some breakfast that way and I won't have to sit here being mad and hungry. I'll buy milk at the store today so I can have cereal tomorrow."

- *Accidents:* After a child spills something, you could say, "At first when that spilled and was starting to drip on me, it felt like it was a really big deal, but then I realized I could make it a little deal by mopping it up—and you helped clean it up. Now I feel much better. Thanks."

- *Child is late for an appointment/activity:* "I am glad to see you today! I had a big Plan A for what we could do together, but I see that we will have less time than I expected, so we need a Plan B. It's your choice, should we drop *A*, *B*, or *C* from what we try to do today?"

- *Child has to be interrupted before completing an activity/work product (try to avoid this situation whenever possible):* You could say, "Can you be flexible and stop that even though you aren't finished?" If yes, then praise flexibility; if no, then say, "I can see that getting interrupted like this is a big deal, but we need to stop now so you can get lunch. Could we make this a little deal by putting your work in a special place on my desk exactly as you have it now, so you can finish it at X *time* today?"

- *Desired item is not available at restaurant:* You might say, "I know this feels like a big deal, but I think there is a way we can turn it into a little deal by picking your second favorite dish and a special dessert. We can also make a plan to come back and get your favorite dish a different day."

- *Desired item is not available in classroom or therapy room:* If the child becomes upset because a favorite book has already been taken by another child or a favorite game or object is missing, you could say, "Boy that is frustrating, I know you wanted X (or I was looking forward to doing Y with you), and now it is not available. Instead of getting stuck on how much fun X or Y would have been, can we be flexible and pick our second-best choice? That way we will at least get part of what we want."

- *Desired item is not available at movies:* If the movie you wanted to see together is sold out, you could say, "I have two ideas for how we can turn this big deal into a little deal. We could pick a different movie, or we could play in the arcade instead of the movie. Do you have a different idea?"

- *Desired item is not available, for example, birthday gift:* If the child does not get the birthday gift he or she wanted from a grandparent, you could say, "I know this feels like a big deal. I have a way I think we can make this into a little deal and not hurt Grandma's feelings. You can say, 'Thank you, Grandma!' Then later we can exchange it for what you want. To do this I need you to stay calm and help me with the plan. Grandma did not want to make you upset. She thought you would like this toy; she did not realize there was one you wanted more."

- *Something goes wrong with something you have worked hard on, for example, cupcakes:* If you spend time making cupcakes and the icing comes out too runny, you could say, "Wow. We have worked hard all morning on these cupcakes and now the icing is wrong and they look terrible. This feels like a really big deal. I think I need to take two deep breaths and then see if I can come up with a Plan B for our cupcakes that makes this a littler deal." (Breathe, pause, breathe.) "Okay, Plan B is I try to thicken the icing with more sugar; if that doesn't work, will you help me with Plan C? We could sprinkle colored sugar on them."

- *Something goes wrong with something you have worked hard on, for example, child's work on a computer is lost:* "You worked really hard on that PowerPoint and put great ideas into it and now the computer has frozen! Is that a big deal or a little deal to you? It feels like a big deal to me. I am going to take two deep breaths and think. What if we call the computer lab and see if they have an idea about how we could get back your PowerPoint?"

- *Something goes wrong with something you have worked hard on, for example, mail order item is not what you expected:* If you order a gift that is clearly too small, you could say, "Oh, man! I spent all this time hunting for just the right sweater for X's birthday and it finally gets here and it is too small, and X's birthday is tomorrow. This feels like a really big deal. Can you help think of a plan to turn it into a little deal?"

- *Creation gets taken apart:* If the child makes elaborate creations and is upset when they have to be taken apart, say, "I don't want this to feel like such a big deal every day when we have to break down the LEGOs. I want to come up with a plan that will make it feel like a littler deal. Tell me if you think this will help: How about every day, we take a picture of your creation, and we create a book of all of the LEGO structures you've made?"

- *When you will be absent from the next school day or therapy session and another person will take your place:* You can say, "Tomorrow/next week I have to go to a doctor's appointment. It is a no-choice for me, so Ms. Z will be your teacher/therapist that day. You may need to be flexible, because she may do some things differently. For instance, she might not make silly jokes like I do, but I think it will just be a little deal, because the important things, like lunch and recess/getting to do a favorite activity will be the same."

- *Making cookies:* While making chocolate chip cookies, you realize that you don't have any chocolate chips. You could say, "We were going to use chocolate chips, but we don't have any. So, we could give up and not make—or eat—any cookies, or we could be flexible and figure out a Plan B. Then we could still eat cookies. What should our Plan B be? Raisins? Nuts? Sugar on top?"

- *Playing a game:* The child wants to go first in a board game, but someone else rolled the higher number. You could ask, "Are you stuck? How can you be flexible and still reach your goal of going first in a game?" Help him or her understand that he or she can go first the next round, which is better than having to stop the game because of not being able to go first in this round.

- *Disagreements between parents:* Your spouse wants to go one place on vacation and you want to go to another. In front of your child, start joking with your spouse, saying, "How about we compromise and do it my way?" Your spouse can then ask if that is how compromise works, and you can talk it through to illustrate how to get to a compromise.

- *On a play date or at indoor recess*: When a child wants to play LEGOs but his or her friend wants to play a board game, say, "How can you be flexible and still reach your goal of having fun with your friend? Can you compromise and play a board game first and then LEGOs? Then you will both get what you want in the end, which is better than not getting what you want at all." When this has been successfully resolved, point out that "being flexible and letting your friend have a turn meant that he or she had fun, so being flexible made you a good friend. That probably means he or she will want to play with you another time."

- *When a child doesn't want to participate in the activity planned:* You could say, "You look stuck right now. My Plan A was to have you do this worksheet so that I would know how much you've learned about shapes. Can we make a compromise so that I can see what you know, but you do it in a way that works for you? Doing just the odd number problems is a really flexible idea!"

- *When you can't find something:* You need a specific pen to review students' journals with them but you can't find it. You can say, "I really need a red pen to mark these journals so that you can see my comments, but I don't have one, so I will be flexible and go to my Plan B, using the green marker today."

- *Food choices:* When a child is stuck because you are out of peanut butter or they got a lunch they didn't like, you can say, "What is your Plan B? Will you have a turkey sandwich, a cheese sandwich, or something else?" or "Let's make a Plan B to let your parents know what you want in your lunch tomorrow."

- *Activity choices:* You can say, "I know you wanted to do Y next, but Sam has already picked Y. Instead of getting stuck on wanting Y, do you have a Plan B choice? That way you will still get to enjoy free time."

- *Unpopular tasks:* If you got a parking ticket, you could say, "Oh, how I wish paying this parking ticket was a choice situation."

- *Disruptive activities:* If a fire drill falls during a preferred class, you could say, "I wish this were a choice situation, but it is a no-choice for all of us."

- *When a document doesn't print the way you expected it to:* "This printer is awful! It feels like such a big deal when my document comes out wrong. Let me take a deep breath and see if I can make this a little deal." Pause and say to the child, "This isn't working. Do you have any suggestions for how I can make this a little deal?"

- *At the store:* A certain toy costs more than you want to spend (or more than your child's allowance). If your child is stuck on the expensive toy, you could say, "I like that toy too, but we can't afford it. If we stay stuck on it, we won't get anything we want. Let's be flexible and find another toy we like, so we end up with something instead of nothing." Suggest another toy within the price range.

- *Bad traffic:* During a traffic jam, you mention that you are feeling stuck and wonder how to feel unstuck. Thinking flexibly (and out loud!), you consider taking a different way home, or taking advantage of being stuck in traffic as an opportunity to play a word game, listen to music, or make up a story. Make each step in your thinking and feeling process explicit by saying it out loud. Encourage the child to help you brainstorm other solutions.

- *When something breaks:* "I think we can make this a little deal by replacing it with another one (or fixing it)."

- *When you make a mistake while doing a chore or errand:* You take the bus all the way to the bank before realizing that you left the check that you need to deposit on the kitchen table. "Let's be flexible and come up with a Plan B." Help the child see your mistake as an "opportunity" for a different solution. "Since we're here, why don't we stop by the library and get a book to look at on the ride home. See, we can make that mistake into a little deal."

TIP

The Key to Avoiding Pitfalls Is to Know that You Cannot Avoid All Pitfalls

We are all humans and we all make mistakes. The most powerful thing you can do to teach a child to admit to mistakes is to admit to them yourself. Then you can turn your mistake into a teaching moment. For example, a child is upset about something and you say, "Don't be silly, that is a little deal, not a big deal," which makes him or her even more upset. Don't despair—you can repair this situation by saying, "I am sorry. I made a mistake. That is not a little deal to you at all, it is a big deal." Pause here and only proceed if the child has calmed down. "Is there a way we could turn it into a little deal?"

HOW TO MAKE IT FUN

Don't forget to have fun with flexibility. Use humor whenever possible. Laugh at yourself, and the child will find it easier to laugh at him or herself. Allow both of you to be silly and creative when learning flexibility. Also do everything in your power to keep it positive. Here are some suggestions:

- *Label "choice" situations more frequently than you label "no-choice" situations:* "You have a choice here."

- *Praise the child for being flexible whenever you can:* "I know you expected pizza, and I love how flexible you're being with the change in plans." "You are more flexible than a rubber band!"

- *Try not to embarrass or shame the child by cuing flexibility in public.* Having a secret, visual "flexibility sign" (see next section on Key Visual and Technological Supports) can help you to unobtrusively remind him or her of the flexibility vocabulary, or use a code word for flexibility, such as *Gumby,* and ask, "Where is Gumby?"

- *Praise the child whenever he or she uses a flexibility script or word.* You can praise with your words, a visual signal (e.g., thumbs up), or by dropping a coin or marble in a jar, which, when full, is used to get a reward.

- *Make "no choice" impersonal, not your decision.* "You know this is one of those no-choice situations. I wish I had control over it, but I don't."

- *Let the child help you be flexible,* even if it is annoying or slow at first.

- Once a child knows these scripts, *always ask before giving your opinion:* "Is this choice or no choice?" "Do you have a Plan B?" "Is this a big deal or a little deal?"

- *Use these scripts to praise and instruct, not to criticize.* Instead of saying, "You are stuck!" ask, "Are you stuck?" or "How can we be flexible about this?"

- *Look for flexibility in others* while watching comedies or cartoons together. Laugh at the character's inflexibility or flexibility (but not at the child, of course).

- *Find examples of heroes being flexible.* Children often admire characters from literature, television, or real life (e.g., Abraham Lincoln, Pikachu, Albert Einstein, Mario). Use examples of what the character does to illustrate flexibility. Talk about how flexible thinking has helped your own heroes, yourself, or your family members. Ask, "What would (child's hero) do?"

- -

KEY VISUAL AND TECHNOLOGICAL SUPPORTS

One way to make sure everyone in the household, school, and therapy settings consistently uses the same flexibility vocabulary and scripts is to post them in a central place at each location (home, school, therapy room), such as a refrigerator, bulletin board, lunch room, bathroom, or next to a computer. The most important visual for this chapter and Chapters 4 and 5 is the Unstuck and On Target! Key Words and Scripts chart, Figure 3.1. We suggest that you post this in a prominent place so that it is always visible. Other ideas for visual supports you may find helpful include the following:

- Everyone involved with the child can use a *flexibility sign,* like a hand signal, a key phrase, or a head tilt, to cue each other when there is an opportunity to be flexible.

- *Set a group* (e.g., family, classroom, therapy group) *goal for flexibility.* Every time someone is flexible, you can record a point. Tally until you reach your goal number on a visual tracking system, such as a drawing of a thermometer (like the United Way pledge thermometer) or a jar you fill with marbles or pennies. Once you reach that goal, do something special together to celebrate being flexible. Some children like to have flexibility parties, with flexible things to eat (e.g., licorice) or do (e.g., obstacle courses).

- When you come to an impasse with a child, experiment with *visual problem-solving charts.* You can draw a simple compromise chart, like the one shown in Figure 3.2, on a whiteboard

I feel/want:	Mom feels/wants:	Compromise:

Figure 3.2. Simple compromise chart.

or a piece of paper and fill it in, making sure that the compromise you come up with allows each person to get some of what he or she wants.

 **PUTTING IT INTO ACTION**
Making
Flexibility Scripts a Habit

Do you feel happy with the way and amount that you are modeling the flexibility vocabulary?

If the answer is yes, congratulations!

If the answer is no, here are some pointers on how to develop a new habit: using flexibility words and phrases. Changing behavior and making a new habit is not easy—many components are involved. You need to do the following:

1. *Have the goal to make flexibility scripts a habit.* If you don't like the words we have suggested or they feel unnatural to you, you may need to come up with your own words for similar ideas that you do like. If you hate the idea of talking out loud about your thinking and feelings, you may need to enlist the help of a family member, teacher, or therapist to do this.

2. *Imagine yourself using the scripts.* Can you think of a time recently when you or the child got frustrated? Was there any part of that frustration that was related to being inflexible? Can you replay that interaction in your head using the flexibility language to imagine a different outcome?

3. *Believe that the flexibility scripts will work.* We have used these scripts in the clinic and classroom for almost 10 years and have repeatedly heard from families that they work. Scripts like Choice/No Choice and Plan A/Plan B have been called "magical" in their ability to reframe situations and reduce conflict. We have also completed a scientific study, published in a peer-reviewed journal, that found that the school curriculum based on these scripts increased flexibility, on-task behavior, ease of making transitions from one thing to another, rule following, and other important skills in children with ASD at home and at school.[11] However, if these scripts don't sound convincing or useful to you, they won't work, even if you try your best to use them. In that case, you may want to talk to other family members, a therapist, a special

educator, or another member of the child's treatment team about whether they think these might work, or if there are ways to adapt them to create something that you can believe in.

4. *Create cues to remind yourself to use the scripts.* Visual reminders help most people. If posting the Key Words and Scripts chart (Figure 3.1) isn't enough, use sticky notes, program reminders into your cell phone, or ask a colleague or your spouse to cue you. If you are using the scripts but no one else in the child's life is, have you given a copy of the Key Words and Scripts chart to others (e.g., grandparents, teachers, therapists, coaches, scout leaders)?

5. *Make a plan to use the scripts.* Think of times in the future when you can predict flexibility problems. They may be specific times in your daily routine (e.g., making the transition from recess back to schoolwork or from snack to homework, getting out of bed in the morning and ready for school) or upcoming special events (e.g., field trip, party, doctor visit, visitor coming to your house) that are likely to create flexibility issues. Can you use any of the flexibility words to prepare the child for the event and model the best outcome in these situations? Try to review for yourself and the child what the challenge and solution might be using flexibility words.

6. *Identify barriers.* For example,

   a. *Does the child cover his or her ears when you use flexibility words?* Don't give up. Remember that this is a new skill for him or her too, and change is not his or her specialty. Keep trying to use the words. If you decide that you are truly stuck, then consider whether collaborating with the child to pick new words might help. Or maybe you need to consult with the rest of the child's treatment team about how to make the intervention more appealing.

   b. *Is the child not motivated to be flexible?* You may need to create a simple visual reward system—for ideas, see Putting It into Action: Setting Up a Reward System in Chapter 6. You could also work with a therapist, teacher, or parent to discuss with the child how being more flexible might help him or her get something he or she wants, and also how being stuck is getting in the way of goals that are important to the child. As we discuss in Chapters 4 and 5, big-picture thinking and goals are not intuitive to many individuals with ASD, and they sometimes need to identify goals in a step-by-step fashion.

On Target
Planning to Achieve Your Goals

Most of us know that we are more likely to get what we want if we can identify what it is that we want to accomplish (goal setting) and can take steps to achieve our goal (planning). We also know that knowing this isn't enough, some of us are better at this than others, and some goals are particularly hard to reach. Goal setting and planning are often difficult for people with ASD, but making the steps to identify and achieve goals explicit can help a lot. This chapter will guide you in teaching these important life skills.

WHAT ARE GOAL SETTING AND PLANNING, AND WHY ARE THEY IMPORTANT?

Goal setting is the ability to identify a goal. Some goals are small (e.g., get dressed, make dinner, clean a room), and others are big (e.g., graduate college, lose weight, make friends). This chapter teaches you how to teach a child a script called Goal, Plan, Do, Check (GPDC)[12] that gives him or her a routine to always follow to stay on target. By teaching the child to set goals and make realistic plans, you will increase his or her ability to follow directions, complete a multistep task, and be an active, independent, and flexible problem solver at school, at home, and with friends. Furthermore, you will also increase his or her self-esteem: the child will feel good when he or she reaches his or her goals. You will feel better too, because by helping the child learn how to stay on target, you reduce the amount of time you spend micromanaging his or her activities, which in turn allows you to be on target with your own goals!

TIP

Great News . . . You Already Use Goal, Plan, Do, Check in Your Everyday Life!

We are constantly making plans and revising them. Imagine going to the grocery store for the ingredients for a spaghetti dinner.

Goal: Buy ingredients for spaghetti dinner.

Plan: Make list. Go to the grocery store. Use shopping list to go down aisles of grocery store to get ingredients.

Do: Here's where things might get messy. You wanted to make spaghetti, but they're all out. Do you melt down because they don't have spaghetti? No—you make a Plan B!

Plan B: Substitute rigatoni for spaghetti.

Check: Are you a bad person because the store did not have spaghetti? No, the problem was the plan—it assumed spaghetti would be available (a reasonable assumption, albeit wrong in this case). So you were flexible, made a Plan B, and moved on. In addition, you were persistent and felt good about the fact that you accomplished your goal.

WHAT ARE THE KEY WORDS AND SCRIPTS OR PHRASES?

This chapter teaches a four-step routine for success with any multipart, short- or long-term task: GPDC. This problem-solving script provides a way to break down any task into small, achievable chunks. It also provides a familiar routine for approaching new and unfamiliar problems or challenges.

Goal

Goals should be specific and meaningful for the child. They can be long-term or big goals, such as, "I want to be able to tie my shoes by myself," "I want to be a computer programmer," "I want to be able to make pancakes by myself," "I want to make a friend to play with at recess," or "I want to get good grades." They can also be short-term or smaller: "I want to go to the new Pixar movie," "I want to invite my friend over for pizza and a game," "I want to get this worksheet finished, so I can have extra time to play on the computer," "I want to have time to read tonight," or "I want to eat lunch with a special friend." If a child has chosen a really large or long-term goal, it may be helpful to break it down into several smaller steps. Use phrases such as the following:

- "This looks like it's something we should make into a goal."
- "I need to set a goal."
- "Let's set a goal!"
- "Do you have a goal?"
- "What is your goal here?"
- "Are you working on your goal?"
- "My goal is to. . . ."
- "You did a great job making a goal!"
- "That's a terrific goal!"

Plan

No one can reach a goal without a plan, either explicit or implicit. When children are learning how to plan, they need clear, explicit, and specific modeling and guidance. Use phrases such as the following:

- "Let's make a plan!"
- "I need a plan."
- "Let's make a Plan B/Plan C."
- "Are you working on your plan?"
- "Do you have a plan?"
- "This is a big project. Let's make a plan for how to break it down day by day."
- "I'm noticing that (identify a consistently problematic issue). Have you noticed that? Let's make a plan for that!"
- "What is your Plan B?"
- "You are terrific at making plans!"

Do

Once you have identified a goal and a specific plan for achieving that goal, it is time to try it out. Explicitly carrying out the *Do* step is critical. Too often, adults help a child make a plan but then assume the hard work is done and the child should implement the plan on his or her own. This almost never works because it is the "doing" that is often hardest for children with ASD. Remember how hard it was for Johnny to carry out his plan for his morning routine (Table 1.1)? A child may be able to tell you what he or she wants—and needs to do to get it—but when the rubber meets the road, he or she may be found lounging on the couch. The same thing may happen at school. In principle, Johnny liked the idea of studying a hero, but he did not even know he needed a plan for getting the project done, much less how to effectively carry out a plan. Link trying out plans to reward systems you already have in place. Use phrases such as the following:

- "This looks like a great plan! Let's think about when we can try it out."

- "It looks like we'll be doing X on Tuesday—that would be a great time to try out your plan."

- "You made a great plan for how to complete the project. Now let's try your plan out. What is the first step?"

- "This looks like a good time to work on your goal. Let's review your plan and try it out!"

- "Okay, I made my plan, and now I am going to try it out."

- "You did a wonderful job trying out your plan! You're working toward your goal just like (name of child's hero)."

Check

When cooking, it is common to set a goal to make a certain dish for a meal, use a recipe in a cookbook as the plan, and carry out the plan (making substitutions or alterations—Plan Bs—as needed). However, many of us don't consider ourselves completely done until we read back through the ingredient list and check to see if we did it all correctly. When you check in with a child to see how his or her plan worked, you can help him or her make any changes to the plan for the next time. Use phrases such as the following:

- "How did it go?"

- "Okay, now I will check to see if I followed my plan."

- "On a scale of 1 to 3, where 1 means 'did not work,' 2 means 'kind of worked,' and 3 means 'worked great,' how did the plan do?"

- "Is there a part of the plan that seemed to work well? Is there part that did not work well?"

- "It looks like some parts of the plan are working but other parts aren't. What would you like to change?"

- "You did such a terrific job trying out your plan—did it work?"

- "Great job checking your plan!"

TEACH BY DOING: HOW TO MODEL GOAL, PLAN, DO, CHECK

Look for moments in your day when you can use some of the GPDC vocabulary. You don't have to use all of it at any given time; just help the child see that these concepts help you to solve problems and get things done. Here are a few basic examples of what you might say. See also Putting It into Action: Mission Possible, Clean Room at the end of this chapter.

- *At the grocery store:* "My goal was to have a nice dinner for Grandma tonight, and my plan was to make her favorite pear tart, but these pears are not ripe. I need a Plan B, but I am stuck. Can you help me think of another dessert that Grandma likes?"

- *You run into a problem with equipment during a lesson or therapy session:* "My goal was to teach you about X, and my plan was to show you some neat examples of X on the computer/overhead/Promethean board, but it is not working, so I need Plan B."

- *When leaving for a trip:* "My goal was to turn off all the lights in the house, and my plan was to start in the kitchen and do one room at a time. Could you help me check to see if my plan worked, and go look at the lights in every room to see if I got them all?"

- *Checking to see whether students have followed directions for an assignment:* "The goal was for everyone to learn to write a persuasive paragraph with a clear topic sentence, three supporting facts, and a conclusion, and the plan was for each of you to follow the outline on the board and write a paragraph arguing for or against daily physical education. Raise your hand if you have completed the plan. Great! Everyone has completed the plan—now let's check. Raise your hand if you have a topic sentence in your paragraph." (Continue to ask about other parts of the plan.) "Did this plan work for you?"

- *Running errands:* "My goal was to finish all my errands today so I can just relax tomorrow, and my plan was to do the grocery shopping, go to the post office, get my prescription filled, and get home in time to run before dinner. Now it is 5 p.m., and I have only completed the first two steps of my plan. Can you help me come up with a Plan B?"

- *Returning students' work to them:* "My goal was to have all your tests graded by this morning so I could give them back to you, and my plan was to finish grading them last night after dinner, but then I had unexpected guests drop by. Now my Plan B is to grade the tests tonight and turn them in tomorrow. Let's see if I am better at carrying out my plan tonight than I was last night!"

- *Paying bills:* "My goal was to pay all the bills before the end of each month, and my plan was to sit down every Sunday and pay all the bills that came that week, but I keep forgetting. I think I need a Plan B with a reminder I can see. Maybe I should make a note in my calendar."

- *Losing weight:* "My goal was to lose 10 pounds before Christmas, and my plan was to lose one pound every week by not eating sweets. But I am not carrying out my plan."

- *Playing at recess:* "Your goal is to have a good time playing tag with your friends. Let's make a plan about what to do when you get tagged and you worry that someone has hit you on purpose."

- *Spouse wants to go out with old friends:* "If your goal is to meet all of your friends on Saturday night, you need to plan to make a reservation or get there early, because you know how crowded it gets there."

- *Child is resisting homework:* "You had a goal of getting an A in math, right? Wasn't part of the plan for achieving that goal doing your homework? Let's check the online grades and see how your plan is working since you've been doing your homework."

- *Child is moping about being asked to clean his or her room:* "If your goal is to get outside and play with your friends, then let's make a plan for getting your room cleaned super-fast. Should we set a timer and make it a race?"

- *Child is having a difficult transition from art to math:* "Your goal is to finish this picture and avoid math. I know math is a hard subject for you. Let's make a plan that both lets you finish your picture later and lets you learn the math you need to know. If we get the math done super quickly and correctly, you can use the extra time to work on your picture!"

The examples that follow are more complex and require a conversation. Some parents, therapists, and teachers find it helpful to use GPDC to solve problems or build routines for getting multistep tasks done, which is what these examples are intended to do. Others prefer just to use the GPDC words when they come up naturally in conversation. Either approach is fine. Appendix A contains sample GPDCs for common problems.

- *Picking a movie for family movie night:* "Our goal is to choose a movie for the family. Let's plan how we're going to pick a movie. How will we know what movie each person wants to watch? . . . That's a great idea: we can ask them. What is our plan for how we will decide if we don't all agree on a movie? . . . You're right: we can vote. And what is our Plan B if everyone wants to watch a different movie or if there is a tie? . . . This is a super plan, let's try it and see if it works."

- *Teaching a new skill in class (e.g., long division):* "Our goal for today's math class is to learn how to do long division (write Goal: Learn Long Division on blackboard). Our plan for this goal has five steps (write on blackboard: Plan: 1] Talk about what long division is, 2] Do three sample long division problems on the board, 3] Make a list of the steps you need to follow to do a long division problem, 4] Try three problems on your own at your desk, 5] Whole class reviews the problems together). Okay let's do our plan." After completing the plan: "Okay, now let's check to see if we achieved our goal. Raise your hand if you think you understand long division now."

- *Before a playdate:* "What is the big goal for your playdate today? That your friend will want to come and play with you again? Let's make a plan. First let's plan what you guys will do together. We should have at least three choices. What is one thing you might do together? . . . Okay, so playing outside is one thing—we need two more. . . . All right, playing LEGOs is another one. What is a third? Can you think of something that your friend likes to do? . . . She likes puzzles; that's great! That's our third choice. We can be flexible and include puzzles on the list, so your friend will have a good time and want to come back. We also need to plan who gets to pick the first activity, and the rule for playdates is that the guest picks first." After the playdate ends: "Let's check to see if we reached our goal. I'm so proud of you for playing puzzles with your friend, because it's something that she likes to do. It looked like you and she had a great time. I bet she'll want to come back over for another playdate sometime."

- *A plan for sharing:* "I see that you and Sammy are having trouble sharing the LEGOs, but I also see that there are plenty of LEGOs for both of you to build something. I want to help you think of a plan so that you can both get at least part of what you want. Our goal is for you to share the LEGOs so that you can both build something cool. Can you think of a way that you can use the LEGOs that is fair to both of you? . . . You can take turns—that is a great idea. Do you think you should be able to choose four or five LEGOs at each turn? Let's make a Plan B for if Sammy chooses a LEGO that you wanted. Let's try out your plan!" Later: "Now let's check in: how did the plan work?"

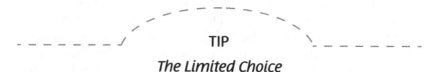

TIP

The Limited Choice

A limited choice is a way for you to share more control with a child while still keeping the activity within helpful boundaries. In the example

- -

about sharing the LEGOs, a child may want to select 20 LEGOs on his turn, almost nullifying the turn-taking exchange. Instead, a child is provided with a choice between two options: four or five LEGOs. Both are acceptable given the activity, but the choice provides a child with more control.

- -

- *Planning to play (and maybe lose) a game:* "So you want to play Uno with your friend when he comes over (or during recess)? What is your goal for the game? . . . To win the game? Tell me this: can you play Uno by yourself? . . . So if you need other people to play with you, then you need to get another person to want to keep playing with you, right? So, what about making this goal for playing Uno: to have fun by playing a game and acting in a way that makes your friend want to play with you again? You may win, but you may need to share the fun of winning with the other person. Let's make a plan for if you win and one for if you lose. For Plan A, let's say you win, what do you need to do? . . . Right. Try not to make the other person feel bad. Maybe your plan could be to say, 'I won, but you might win next time.' If you lose, your Plan B could be to say to yourself, 'I lost, but I had fun playing and maybe I will win next time.'" After the game is over: "Let's check how your plan worked. Did you meet the goal of having fun and acting in a way that made your friend want to play Uno with you again?"

- *Morning routine:* "I've noticed that our mornings aren't very fun. Do you like how the mornings have been going? . . . How about setting a goal that you can get yourself ready without my help each morning before the bus arrives? If you are able to get ready quickly on your own, then you will have time to read before the bus comes. Let's make a plan: 1) Wake up—what is the best plan for you waking up fast? (discuss options such as alarm, music, curtains open), 2) Get dressed (if this is slow, then discuss starting the plan with laying clothes out the night before), 3) Eat breakfast, 4) Brush teeth, 5) Put backpack and coat by front door (backpack can also be set up the night before)." Later: "Let's check and see if our Plan A worked. . . . One thing I noticed was that I needed to keep telling you what you should have been doing. How about a Plan B where we use a written-down checklist instead? (See Appendix A for a sample morning routine GPDC.)

- *Making transitions between classes:* "I've noticed that you have a hard time moving from one class to the next. It seems like you are struggling to finish up what you want to work on, and that makes you late for the next subject—so then you have to play catch-up. Let's make a plan to have smoother transitions—it seems like a good goal so you don't feel so overwhelmed. What if we give you a special timer that lets you know 5 minutes before the end of the class that it's time to look for a stopping point. You can use those 5 minutes to wrap up, and when the teacher tells the rest of the class, "Time's up," you'll be ready to go—and get to be one of the first students in line! If you're not done, we can make a plan for you to finish during lunch with me if you like." When you've tried out the transition plan, check in when the student and ask, "How did you like this plan? Do we need to make any changes so it goes more smoothly?"

- *Turning in homework:* "I know that you want to become a video game programmer when you grow up. You have to do really well in school in order to become a video game programmer. In order to do well in school, you have to turn in your homework. How does a goal of turning in all your homework on time sound to you? . . . Okay, then let's make a plan: 1) Bring everything you need home from school, 2) Do your homework at home, 3) Take all your finished homework back to school, 4) Turn it in to your teacher. Does that cover it? Let's try it out." Later at school, the teacher can remind the student to check his checklist and show him where the homework turn-in bin is located. Later at home: "Let's check to see how your homework plan worked." This is a difficult problem and will require lots of plans to get it right; see the Tip: Independent Class and Homework Strategies for some troubleshooting ideas and remember to provide the child with a written checklist or routine to follow. Also find another homework GPDC model in Appendix A.

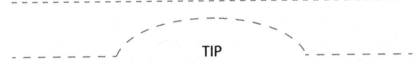

TIP

Independent Class and Homework Strategies

There are many possible Plan Bs, Cs, and Ds you can use in order to fine-tune the independent work or homework routine. Actively use the check procedure to check in on what is working and what isn't. Here are possible solutions to some common issues:

- If a child can't stick with work without a visual reminder that it won't last forever, make a plan that includes using a timer so he or she can see there will be a break when it dings.

- If a child can't follow the directions or steps you give him or her to complete the work, try writing the plan or steps down on a whiteboard so he or she can refer to it.

- If it is hard for the child to return to work after taking a break, or if the child needs multiple little breaks, you can create a plan that involves putting together a schedule with specific times for homework and breaks.

- If a child is bothered by too much noise, make a plan with a new location for where he or she can work. Or you can make a plan to use headphones or earplugs.

- If a child chronically underestimates how long an assignment will take, build predicting how long it will take into the plan—and make sure to check the accuracy of the prediction when you do the Check at the end.

- If a child struggles to bring the right materials home or turn in homework even with a checklist, then the Plan B may be to create a home and school routine that is the same every day to make sure homework is communicated, completed, and returned. Making a plan that straddles home and school can be a very powerful tool—and a perfect opportunity to collaborate across settings. Consider making a laminated checklist or other communication device.

- *Completing independent work in class:* "I know that you want to become a paleontologist when you grow up. You have to do really well in school in order to become a paleontologist. In order to do well in school, you have to finish your schoolwork. How does a goal of finishing your assignments on time sound to you? . . . Okay then let's make a plan: 1) Listen to and read the instructions; 2) Stop and think. Do they make sense to you? Do you have everything you need to complete the task? If not, ask for help; 3) When you finish the task, check to make sure you didn't skip anything and that you put your name on the paper; 4) Turn the work in to your teacher. Does that cover it? Let's try it out." Later: "Let's check to see how your schoolwork plan worked." This is a difficult problem and will require lots of plans to get it right; see the Tip: Independent Class and Homework Strategies for some troubleshooting ideas, and remember to provide the child with a written checklist or routine to follow.

- *Making a meal:* "Our goal is to make spaghetti and meatballs together. Do we have everything we'll need? Let's make a plan to check the ingredient list on the recipe and write down things we need to get at the store; then we can use the recipe for the rest of our plan. . . . Great! We made a list, checked it, went to the store, and got everything we needed. Now let's read the recipe carefully and use it to plan all the next steps we need to follow." Later: "Now let's check. How did the plan work? You did a great job checking the list at the store and following the recipe. Look around the kitchen: did we leave off a step of cleaning up? . . . How would you change the plan the next time?"

- *Keeping room clean:* "I've noticed that sometimes your room gets so messy that it is hard for you to find things you want. Have you noticed that? . . . Should we make a goal for you learn to clean your room really fast so you can go do fun stuff *and* find your things when you need them? . . . Okay, here's a plan to help you reach your goal in four steps: 1) Pick a time every day when you have some free time. . . . After snack? That sounds great; 2) Pick up all the clothes that are not put away and then dump dirty clothes in the hamper and put clean clothes in your dresser; 3) Put all your toys in the toy box; 4) Put your books on your nightstand or on the bookshelf. What do you think? . . . How fast do you think you can do this plan? 10 minutes? Let's set the timer and see. Okay, the timer went off, let's check in: Are your clothes put away? Yes! Are your toys put away? Yes! What about your books? Yes! And you did it all before the timer went off. Great job! Let's write down your plan and post it in your room so you can look at it each day when you clean up." See Putting It into Action: Mission Possible, Clean Room at the end of this chapter.

HOW TO MAKE IT FUN

GPDC is a complicated script that takes effort to learn. Both you and the child will feel frustrated and overwhelmed if you try to teach both the script and a difficult skill at the same time. Remember that just using the terms *goal, plan, do,* and *check* when you talk about your own decisions and actions is enough. You don't have to make up elaborate routines if you don't want to. Also, give yourself permission to be silly. Use the child's special interest or hero in the GPDC. For example, he or she may want his or her room to be as clean as his or her hero's house, laboratory, or workspace. Use humor in the GPDC: "My goal is to have a clean room so I don't get lost in all my stuff," or "Look around my room for all trash, fish, small animals, and other uninvited guests." Following the child's work on a GPDC, give him or her an opportunity to engage in a preferred activity, especially if it makes everyone laugh and/or have fun.

KEY VISUAL AND TECHNOLOGICAL SUPPORTS

The most important visual for this chapter is the Unstuck and On Target! Key Words and Scripts, Figure 3.1. We suggest that you post this on your bulletin board, refrigerator, lunch room, computer, bathroom mirror, or some other prominent place so that it is always visible. Copies should also be posted at home and school and in any therapy settings the child attends. When creating GPDCs, you can write them down. Let the child dictate if writing is difficult for him or her. Keep a copy of a helpful GPDC someplace where the child can see it and refer to it when engaging in the activity (e.g., a copy of a "clean your room" GPDC should be posted in his or her room or a copy of "preparing a meal" GPDC should be in the kitchen). Figures 4.1, 4.2, and 4.3 provide some different examples of visuals. Many children like the "Mission Possible" format (Figure 4.3). You can add images of a child's special interest to help him or her feel more connected to the GPDC.

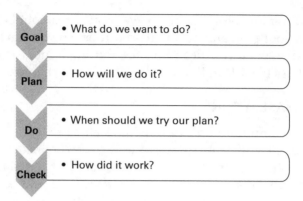

Figure 4.1.   Sample Goal, Plan, Do, Check worksheet. (*Source:* Cannon, 2011.)

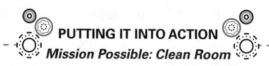 **PUTTING IT INTO ACTION**
Mission Possible: Clean Room

Identify something that you think would be useful to formally write out as a GDPC. Pick one of the Teach by Doing: How to Model Goal, Plan, Do, Check examples given earlier in this chapter or use your own example. Use one of the visual templates in Figures 4.1, 4.2, or 4.3, or make your own. Use the example in Figure 4.4 and the sample checklist in Figure 4.5 if they help you get started.

Basic Goal, Plan, Do, Check Worksheet

Goal:

Plan:

Do:

Check:

Figure 4.2. Basic Goal, Plan, Do, Check Worksheet. (*Source:* Cannon, 2011.)

Mission Possible
Goal, Plan, Do, Check

Goal: *What do you want to do?*

_____

_____

_____

Plan A: *How do you want to do it?* _____

_____

_____

_____

_____

Plan B: *How do you want to do it if Plan A doesn't work?*

_____

_____

_____

_____

_____

Do: *When do you want to try out your plan?* _____

_____

_____

_____

_____

Check: *Did your plan work?* Yes/No

What was most helpful? _____

_____

_____

_____

_____

_____

Figure 4.3. Mission Possible: Goal, Plan, Do, Check worksheet.

Mission Possible
Goal, Plan, Do, Check

Goal: *What do you want to do?*

Keep my room clean.

_____

Plan A: *How do you want to do it?* _____

Put clothes away

    • Clean clothes in the closet

    • Dirty clothes in the hamper

Put toys in toy box.

Put books on bookshelf.

When I finish cleaning my room, I get to play a game with Mom.

Do: *When do you want to try out your plan?* _____

I will create a checklist of my plan and do the plan every day
after snack, checking off my checklist as I go. Every time that I
do my plan, I get to play a game with Mom.

_____

Check: *Did your plan work?* (Yes)No

Do I need to add any steps to the checklist?

_____

Figure 4.4. Mission possible: Clean room Goal, Plan, Do, Check sample. (From Cannon, L., Kenworthy, L., Alexander, K.C., Werner, M.A., & Anthony, L.G. [2011]. *Unstuck and on target!: An executive function curriculum to improve flexibility for children with autism spectrum disorders, research edition* [pp. 140, 143]. Baltimore, MD: Paul H. Brookes Publishing Co.; adapted by permission.)

Mission Possible
Clean Room Checklist

Steps to a clean room	Check it off!
1. Pick up clothes	
2.	
3.	
4.	
5.	
6.	
7.	
8.	
9. Get my reward!	

Figure 4.5. Mission Possible: Clean Room Checklist.

Target Goal

In this chapter, you will learn to teach how to set priorities, identify distractors, and monitor progress. The balance between working toward a goal and giving in to whims is a difficult one, because we all like to have fun in the moment. The skills in this chapter will help those with ASD make conscious choices about when to work toward a goal and when to just have fun.

WHAT IS A TARGET GOAL, AND WHY IS IT IMPORTANT?

A *target goal* is something that you want or need to do that is more important than anything else you may want to do at the same time. Children with ASD often have difficulty determining what is most important in a situation. They can easily lose sight of the big picture and become distracted by smaller details. For this reason, it is important to help children select overarching goals: target goals that may take a long time to achieve. They need explicit instruction and support in distinguishing between their target goals and smaller, more immediate goals that can interfere with the target goal. Each day, in every situation, consciously or unconsciously, we are working toward one or more target goals and are simultaneously faced with smaller goals, wants or desires, or "whims" that could steer us off target.

TIP

Distinguishing Between Target Goals and Whims

Target Goal: You set and work toward target goals on a daily basis (e.g., to be a good parent or teacher or therapist, to make it to work on time).

- -

These goals are overarching in nature, may include multiple steps, and often take a long time to achieve (i.e., work toward some goals—such as being healthy, being a good student, getting a 3.5 grade point average, or maintaining a friendship—must be sustained over many years).

Whims: You are constantly presented with whims that may or may not be in conflict with your target goal (e.g., turning off the alarm clock and going back to sleep when your target goal is to get to work on time). When you are faced with a whim, you have to make some decisions: Is it important enough to me to disrupt progress toward my target goal? Can I modify my whim so that it does not disrupt my target goal?

- -

Whims are defined as distractors that can interfere with reaching a target goal. We often have to choose between target goals and whims. For example, your target goal might be to lose weight. A co-worker is celebrating her birthday and offers you a piece of cake. Your whim (or immediate objective) is to enjoy a piece of cake and celebrate with your friend; this has the potential to derail your target goal of losing weight.

To illustrate this concept for children, you can ask them to visualize an arrow moving through space toward a big target. A whim is anything that diverts the arrow from the target. If *whim* isn't a word that works well with the child, please feel free to customize the language to be more meaningful to you and the child. Some examples of modifications include substituting "off target" for *whim* and introducing the idea of "on target" and "off target." When the child is on target, the dart is heading straight for the bull's-eye; when he or she is off target, tempted by a distractor or whim, the dart is heading for the edge or off the board. If sports resonate with your child, you can substitute "target goals" with "keeping your eye on the ball," and "whim" with all of the distractions that happen while you are playing (e.g., fans, noise, another player moving, an ice cream cone).

Because children with ASD have trouble seeing the big picture and integrating information, they are easily distracted by whims—leading them off target. Sometimes, they are unable to understand what the target goal is. They require explicit instruction about the concept of a target goal and initially need help identifying their target goal in a given situation. Then they need to be taught how to set target goals, recognize that some goals are more important than others, identify when smaller goals take them off target, and determine how to modify or let go of their whim so that it is not in conflict with their target goal.

The concept of a target goal is a tool for helping children to identify the most important goal in a given situation. Once a child understands that, he or she will be much less likely to get "lost in the weeds" and derailed from important activities. The concept of a whim is a tool for helping children identify when something they want or a desire is less important than their target goal (even though the whim can feel important at the time) when it risks compromising the success of the target goal. The language related to target goals and whims can remind children that the target goal is ultimately more important than the whim and, therefore, make them more willing to modify or let go of the whim to continue to work toward their target goal. It gives you a shorthand for helping children marshal all of their self-control to meet an important goal, such as making a friend, writing an essay, or participating in recess while delaying or suppressing a whim or desire. That, in turn, makes your life easier, because the child will be better at sticking to his or her goals without your assistance.

WHAT ARE THE KEY WORDS AND SCRIPTS OR PHRASES?

In this chapter, you will continue to use and build on the language you learned in Chapter 4: Goal, Plan, Do, Check. You will learn how to help a child distinguish big, important target goals from smaller, less important whims, which sometimes distract people from target goals and get them off target. You will also learn how to help a child choose between two goals or desires in favor of the more important target goal, thereby helping a child to "keep his or her eye on the ball." The new phrases to use are the following:

- "Are we on target?"

- "What is your goal?"

- "A goal is something you want or need to do."

- "What is your target goal?"

- "Is that a target goal or a whim?"

- "I can see you really want to keep X as your friend. I think your target goal is to be a good friend."

- "Are you on target right now?"

- "I know this is fun, but do you think it is getting us off target?"

- "I know this is fun; let's plan another time to do it so it does not get in the way of our target goal."

- "I know you really want to be a video game programmer. If this is your target goal, what are the things you need to do to accomplish this goal?"

- "Oh man, I got so off target just then!"

- "Let's stay on target until we reach our goal; then we can take a break and do X."

- "Is that your target goal or is that a whim?"

- "Great job choosing your target goal to X."

- "Way to stay on target!"

- "You just figured out a way to accomplish that whim at a different time so that it did not get in the way of your target goal."

- "You just ignored a whim that was exciting! Excellent job staying on target!"

- "You ignored something that you really wanted so that you could keep your eyes on the ball—excellent work!"

- "I can tell that you really wanted X, but you chose to stay on target, and that will help you get something even more important more quickly!"

Alternative Language for Target and Whim Scripts

Target goal

- On target
- Aim for the target.
- Big goal
- Main goal

- Central goal
- Big picture
- On track
- Keep your eyes on the prize.
- Keep your eye on the ball.

Whim

- Want or desire
- Little goal
- Off target
- Off track/derailment
- Distraction/distractor

TEACH BY DOING: HOW TO MODEL STAYING ON TARGET

Often, you can point out in yourself when a whim is getting in the way of a target or help a child *ignore, postpone,* or *modify* a whim until a target is reached (e.g., "I really want to play my new video game, but I have homework, and my target goal is to get good grades": *ignore* = skip playing video games, *postpone* = play after I am done with my homework, *modify* = play 10 minutes now and for half an hour after my homework is done). The following are examples of modeling these scripts:

- *When you do chores before you indulge a whim:* "My target goal is to clean the house, and my whim is to watch my favorite television show. I want to make sure I accomplish my target goal, so I am going to start cleaning the house earlier so I will be finished by the time my show comes on."

- *When the class discussion is going off on a tangent:* "Let's stay on target and finish talking about X" or "I don't want to get too far off target. Let's focus on X."

- *When you have gotten derailed by a whim while making dinner:* "Oops! My target goal was to make dinner, but here I am checking my e-mail. I guess that is a whim that I should only work on after I finish making dinner. What do you think?"

- *When socializing or a preferred activity gets in the way of class-work:* "I know you mentioned that you really hope to get all A's this quarter. Part of your grade includes getting your classwork turned in on time. Is reading your comic book a whim, or will it help you achieve your target goal? Can you think of another time when reading your book would not get in the way of your target goal?"

- *When you get distracted while shopping:* "Wait a minute: what did we come to the mall for—what was our target goal?" . . . "So eating this ice cream cone right now is a whim, isn't it? Can we eat our ice cream and still get back on track?"

- *When a child is losing sight of a target goal:* "Is that your target goal or is it a whim? I know you really wanted to X: that was a whim. Let's make a plan so you can still do what you want but not let it get in the way of your target goal."

- *Before a playdate or recess:* "What is your target goal for this playdate (recess)?" If no answer or a whim is offered: "What about making sure Elias has a good time so he will want to play with you again? Or what about having Elias become your friend?" . . . "What are whims that could get in the way of your target goal?" If no answer or an inappropriate whim is offered: "What about wanting to go first in every game you play? What about wanting to decide every game that you play? How can you keep your whims from getting you off target?" Help the child think about compromises at this point.

- *When watching TV or reading a book with a child:* As the plot unfolds, begin to identify when the characters are working toward a target goal. Point out when a whim presents itself and how the character responds. Did the character persevere and continue working toward his or her target goal, or did he or she give into the whim?

  Example: SpongeBob's target goal is to make it to the Krabby Patty on time. His best friend, Patrick, shows up at his pineapple and wants to hang out. "What is SpongeBob's target goal? What is the whim?"

  Example: "So Jake's target goal was being a good student and finishing his homework. He had to wait to follow his whim until his homework was done. He wanted to go out and play with his friends and watch television, but those are called *whims*. They are little things that Jake may have wanted to pursue, but they would interfere with his target goal."

- *Explicitly identify the target goal and whim for key times of day when derailments often occur.* For instance, before the child goes to bed, parents could say, "What do you think the target goal is for the morning, before school?" (Or, if your child will have trouble with that question: "My target goal for the morning before school is getting you to school on time and me to work on time.") Write down the goal on a sticky note. Then say, "What whims could get in our way?" You can offer your whims: "I think I might have problems with the whim of wanting to stay in bed after my alarm goes off, or I might want to read the paper and drink my coffee for 15 minutes instead of 10 minutes. I think I will keep my eyes on the prize by hitting the snooze only one time." Then ask your child, "What whims will get in your way? How can you keep your eye on the target goal? . . . Let's write that down to remind us."

- *At school, teachers may want to help a child stay on target during the transition between classes.* You could say, "What do you think your target goal is for switching classes?" or state, "My target goal for switching classes is to be ready for the next class on time with all of the items I need." Use sticky notes, as in the previous example, and probe what could get in the way of the target goal. Offer potential whims: "I think I would get off target with the whim of wanting to talk with my friend. I think I will keep heading toward my target by telling my friend that we can talk later." Then ask your student, "What whims will get in your way? How can you keep your eye on the target goal? Let's write that down to help us remember."

HOW TO MAKE IT FUN

- *Link target goals to your reinforcement system:* Setting goals, both short term and long term, is hard work. Staying on target and working toward your goals in the face of more immediate, smaller goals is even harder work. Include working toward target goals in your existing reinforcement system and provide rewards for achieving goals and avoiding or postponing whims.

- *As often as possible, highlight what is going well.* Offer specific praise and provide encouragement.

- *Link it to a hero:* Use examples of what the child's hero does to illustrate working toward target goals and managing the whims that can possibly derail him or her from achieving target goals. Example: Superman's target goal is to rescue people from the dangerous situation. "What would happen if Superman decided to stop for a donut?" Abraham Lincoln's goal was to end slavery. "What if he decided he wanted to go on vacation and skip signing the Emancipation Proclamation?" When the child faces a hard choice between being on target or indulging a strong whim, ask, "What would (child's hero) do?"

- *Play games with the idea of whim and target goals at home.* For example, Whim Whammy is a car game that can be used to prime children for what they can expect in a new situation and what you will expect from them. It is also a fun way to reinforce the idea of whims and target goals. In the car on the way to the event, determine your target goal. Brainstorm potential whims and your plan for how to keep your eyes on the target goal. Keep track of the number of whims you come up with. Each time, try to come up with more than the time before (i.e., try to beat your score from the ride before). Don't be afraid to be silly!

- *Play games with the idea of whims and target goals at school.* In the classroom, brainstorm potential target and whims prior to an assembly or an extensive classroom activity. It can become a fun way to prepare your entire class for activities.

- *Add goals to other games:* Add target goals when playing board games and make up rewards for achieving them and ignoring or postponing whims. Example: The class is getting ready to play a game of Around the World. Decide the target goal for the game (e.g., to have fun, to be a good sport). Decide what players will win when they do things that help them work toward the target goal. For example, if the target goal is to be a good sport, then a nickel or point could be earned each time a person compliments another player or is calm when his or her turn goes badly.

- *It doesn't have to be all or nothing.* Help your child or student develop an alternative time or place when they can accomplish their whim so that it does not interfere with their target goal: "I know you want to go first right now, but your target goal is to be a good friend. If you let your friend go first right now, you can go first next time."

KEY VISUAL AND TECHNOLOGICAL SUPPORTS

Using visuals serves as a way to document target goals, possible whims, and the plans you create for how to stay on target. These can serve as visual reminders of what the target goal is. It is also possible that some target goals will be the same from day to day (e.g., to get to school on time). The visual for that target goal can stay displayed in a prominent place to support the morning routine. For example:

TARGET GOAL

Morning: to get to school on time

POSSIBLE WHIM

Want to watch a cartoon

PLAN

Record the show to watch later.

PUTTING IT INTO ACTION
Staying on Target

Pick one of the Teach by Doing: How to Model Staying on Target examples given earlier in this chapter, or use your own example. Try it out. Create a visual reminder that will help the child stay on target. Use the visual template in Figure 5.1 if it helps you and the child, or make your own.

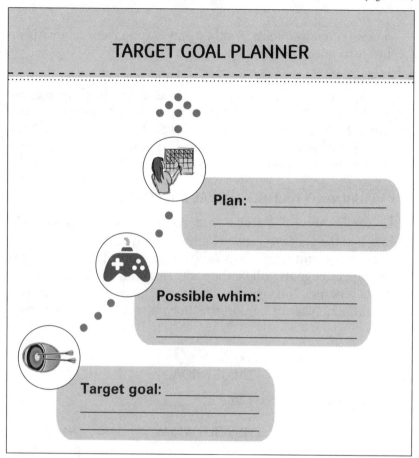

Figure 5.1. Target Goal Planner.

PUTTING IT INTO ACTION
Bringing It All Together

The following case studies are included to give you ideas about how to integrate target goals, as well as previously introduced scripts, into real-life situations. The first case study primarily reviews the skills and scripts discussed in this chapter; additional case studies then go over concepts from throughout this book.

Planning and Navigating a Playdate

Caroline had been waiting to have a playdate with Maria for weeks. It wasn't often that Caroline talked about peers at school, so when Caroline mentioned wanting to have Maria over to her house, her parents wanted to make it happen as soon as possible.

As they prepared for the playdate, Caroline started to outline all of the things she planned to have happen when Maria came over: "First, we will go outside and draw with chalk, then we will play Wii, only Mario Cart, then we will have a snack. . . ." It dawned on Caroline's mother that Caroline's expectations for how the playdate would go were very specific—if Maria had a different agenda or wanted to do something different, the playdate could unravel very quickly. Caroline's mom told Caroline she knew Maria was excited about the playdate and that her target goal was to have fun with her friend, but that Maria may have different ideas or things she wanted to do when she came over. Caroline's mom told her, "If you are not flexible and listen to her suggestions and only pursue your whims, it might upset Maria and get in the way of your target goal. Remember, your target is to have fun with your friend, not to get to do only things you want to do, right?" She suggested they make a GPDC to help plan for the different variations or ways the playdate could go. They came up with a plan for each part of the playdate (Figure 5.2).

At first, things went very well. Maria said she would rather play inside than outside and said Candy Land was her favorite game. The two sat down to play, and Caroline grabbed her favorite blue piece; as luck would have it, that was Maria's favorite piece as well. The two were at a standstill, unable to think of an alternative. Caroline stormed out of the room.

Alone with Caroline in her bedroom, Caroline's mom asked her if this felt like a big deal or a little deal. "*Huge deal!*" screamed Caroline. Caroline's mom said, "Alright, then we need to figure out a way to make

Goal: To have fun with Maria	
Plan A: Ask Maria if she wants to play outside.	Plan B: Ask Maria if she wants to play inside.
Ask Maria if she wants to play with chalk or on the jungle gym.	Ask Maria if she wants to play with playdough or Candy Land.

Figure 5.2. Goal, Plan, Do, Check for Caroline's playdate with Maria.

this a little deal so that you can get back to your goal of having fun with Maria. I think I have an idea. How about a compromise so both people get some of what they want? You both like blue, and it doesn't matter what your blue pieces looks like as long as they look different and you don't get confused on the board. Why don't you take a blue piece from our Sorry game and use that as your piece? Caroline, that would be the choice of a good friend and a flexible choice, and would certainly earn you three marbles for your flexibility jar." Caroline paused for a moment and then quietly agreed. Caroline's mom could see her hesitation and added, "Remember, when you are flexible and make good friend choices, it makes your friend more likely to come back again. I remember you saying that's really important to you—a target goal." Caroline agreed. She and her mom found the Sorry piece so that Caroline could play, and Caroline's mom was happy to find that there was just enough of Caroline's favorite snack left for the girls to share after they finished the game.

Earning a Trip to the Movies

Max had been waiting for weeks to see the new *Harry Potter* movie. Max's mom capitalized on this motivation and used the movie as reinforcement for completing the steps on the responsibility chart he had been working on at home.

Max was working on becoming more independent with his daily routines. This included morning and afternoon routines as well as cleaning up after himself. Each step Max completed independently on his responsibility chart equaled one marble. When the jar was full, he could go see the *Harry Potter* movie. Mom figured this would take about 2 weeks, just in time for the movie premiere. Max's morning responsibility chart is shown in Figure 5.3.

Things were going very well—Max's mom couldn't believe how motivating the movie was. There were a few minor issues: every now

Morning Routine	
Task	**Marble**
❑ Get up when my alarm goes off.	
❑ Brush my teeth.	
❑ Wash my face.	
❑ Put on my clothes.	

Figure 5.3. Max's responsibility chart.

and then, Max would become distracted by something during the morning and lose sight of his steps or refuse to put his dishes in the sink in an attempt to get to his television time faster. At those times, his mother would remind him about the step—Max knew this meant he wasn't going to earn the marble, because he didn't do the task without reminding; he would still be able to earn the marbles for the next steps if he did them without a reminder.

In 2 short weeks, Max filled the jar, and the family made plans to go to the movie. That Saturday, the family loaded into the car and headed to the theater for opening weekend. *Harry Potter* fans all over the world know that this could be a mistake: the movie was sold out long before the family arrived at the theater. Upon discovering this, Max immediately started to panic and was on the verge of a meltdown.

At this point, Max's dad walked Max to a quieter place in the theater and pulled out a pad. Max recognized this as a cue that a plan was going to be made. Max's dad said, "Max, I know this is a huge deal. You did an amazing job earning your marbles and the chance to see *Harry Potter*. Let's create a plan that turns this big deal into a little deal and gets us to our goal of seeing Harry Potter." (See Figure 5.4.)

Homework

Homework has always been a challenge for Ethan. By the time homework time rolls around, he is exhausted from the demands of the day and panicky he won't have time to himself. The worst days are the ones when he has multiple assignments—he just can't figure out how to prioritize them; he becomes easily overwhelmed, and often the result

Goal: To see a *Harry Potter* movie and earn extra marbles for staying calm		
Plan A: See a *Harry Potter* movie today.	Plan B: Play in the arcade for half an hour and buy tickets for tomorrow's showing.	Plan C: Play in the arcade for half an hour and buy tickets for the next open showing.
Do: Try Plan B. If Plan B doesn't work, we will try Plan C.		
Check: Did I accomplish my goal of seeing the *Harry Potter* movie? Did I earn extra marbles for staying calm?		

Figure 5.4.   Making new plans for seeing a *Harry Potter* movie. (*Source:* Cannon, 2011.)

is tears and lots of negotiation. Without exception, getting homework done takes twice as long as it should.

Ethan's dad was tired of the nightly battle over homework and decided to help Ethan think through the homework situation. As they rode home from school one day, they talked about things they like doing and things they don't like doing. They discussed the things they have control over or a choice about and the things they don't have control over that are no-choice situations. Homework is one of those no-choice situations. Ethan's dad asked, "Ethan, do you feel like you have no choice about your homework?" Ethan replied, "Dad, *yes!* They force me to do homework, and I hate it!" Ethan's dad said, "Ethan, I totally understand; sometimes I feel that way about things too, but I make myself feel better with a special trick." Ethan looked puzzled and asked, "What's that?" Ethan's dad smiled and said, "I remind myself of how doing what I don't like will get me something I want—like when we all finish our vegetables at dinner so we can get dessert. Does doing your homework get you something that you want?" Ethan confessed that he likes to do well in school and hates to miss recess when his homework is not done. Ethan's dad shared that if doing well in school and making sure he earns his free time are goals, then doing homework is a difficult choice he can make to get the things he likes. Ethan's dad told him he wanted to create a plan that helped him get through his homework. Ethan's dad decided to create a GPDC and a reward system for the homework routine.

Ethan is a LEGO fanatic; he loves to collect sets and will build with all of his free time. Ethan's dad decided that earning LEGO pieces would be the perfect incentive system for Ethan to complete his homework. Together, Ethan and his dad created a GPDC for the nightly homework routine (Figure 5.5). They talked about which subjects are the hardest, which are the easiest, and what strategies would be helpful to get Ethan through the homework.

Group Work

Jimmy loves science; in fact, when given the opportunity he will regale you with facts about the solar system, dinosaurs, and the periodic table. This year's science class is very hands-on, and each class period the students work through a scientific experiment. Each week, the students are assigned to a group of four students, given a task, and required to work through the scientific method as a group. The students are aware that their grade is not only based on the outcome of the experiment but also on their ability to work together as a group. Jimmy's teacher assumed that, with his background knowledge and love of science, Jimmy would excel in his class. Unfortunately, Jimmy rarely makes it through the assignment without getting upset or giving up, and his classmates are starting to show signs of frustration when he is assigned to their group.

Jimmy's teacher sat down to observe how things were playing out in Jimmy's group. When the group sat down to do the experiment with chemicals, Jimmy quickly launched into a summary of how the chemicals would affect one another. When his peers tried to make alternative predictions, he told them they were wrong and again shared a litany of facts to support his claim. The group then got to work without much discussion of individual jobs. One person picked up the pencil and

---

Goal: To complete my homework and earn LEGO pieces

Plan:

❏ Small snack
❏ Vocabulary exercise (because it is easy and it is the same each night) = 1 LEGO piece
❏ Math = 3 LEGO pieces
❏ Snack/break (10 minutes) = 2 LEGO pieces if I stop on time
❏ Science or social studies = 3 LEGO pieces
❏ Book of the week (save the best for last ☺) = 2 LEGO pieces
❏ LEGO TIME!! ☺

Figure 5.5.   Goal, Plan, Do, Check for Ethan's homework.

began writing the group's thoughts (recorder), one person collected the materials (materials manager), and one person grabbed the workbook and started to lead the group through the steps of the experiment (facilitator). All of the students got straight to work and seemed to know just what to do, except Jimmy. He grew increasingly less interested in the experiment, only chiming in if a group member made a claim that he disagreed with. Once the chemicals had been combined, Jimmy became upset because he had not had a turn, and he left the group to go sit in the back of the classroom.

After observing the group, Jimmy's teacher realized the free-flowing nature of the group dynamic was too difficult for Jimmy to respond to and did not provide him with a clear set of expectations for his own involvement. It also became clear that Jimmy was not aware of how his "all knowing" comments were being perceived. Jimmy's teacher decided that the best way to support Jimmy would be to work with him to create a standard GPDC to follow when conducting an experiment with his classmates. This framework would make clear the step of assigning and identifying group jobs. Jimmy's job would be to walk his group members through the GPDC and check off each step as they completed it. This process ensured that Jimmy remained engaged throughout the whole experiment. During this conversation, Jimmy's teacher also took the opportunity to talk with Jimmy about his reputation within the group. Jimmy was motivated to be with the group, and together they came up with scripts for how he could share information ("I was thinking . . .") and respond to others' ideas ("That is an interesting idea" or "Let's try it out"). They developed a self-monitoring system whereby Jimmy would give himself a check when he let another person share an idea and he was able to provide positive feedback. Once Jimmy earned a certain amount of checks, he earned time to research a science topic of his choice. Finally, Jimmy and his teacher talked about his target goal. Jimmy shared that he is very interested in getting straight A's this quarter. They discussed how some of his other goals, or whims, such as wanting everyone to know everything he knows, were getting in the way of his group participation and his ability to finish the assignment, thereby affecting his grades and target goal. Together they reflected on how his new strategies (GPDC and tally marks) would help him stay on target. Once the GPDC plan was up and running, Jimmy's teacher started to notice how smoothly and efficiently the group was working together. He decided that all of his students could benefit from the GPDC structure. He was pleased to discover how independent the students became and how, within a few short months, they were able to create their own GPDC based on the assignment.

Troubleshooting

Changing the Environment to Solve Everyday Problems

This chapter is designed to help you think about ways you can change the demands on a child if you are facing any of the eight common problems addressed here. Sometimes, trying these solutions will make the Unstuck and On Target! interventions work better. These tips are designed to target many common trouble spots that arise for children with ASD, their families, teachers, and intervention teams.

> **Problem 1:** *"I feel like I am nagging all the time" or "The child and I are both frustrated."*
>
> **Solution:** *Remember to "keep it positive."*

WHY KEEP IT POSITIVE?

This may be the single most powerful message in this book! Just as you teach a child that his or her behavior has consequences, remember that your mood and behavior have consequences, too. Happiness, sadness, anxiety, and frustration are all contagious. Most people smile at the sound of a baby's laughter, even across the room. In that same way, your actions and mood have a profound effect on the child's actions and mood. Positive feelings from you will create more positive feelings in the child. Negative feelings (expressed in yelling, threatening, punishing) from you will increase negative feelings and behaviors in the child. This creates a negative cycle (Figure 6.1), and it feels bad to everyone (see Gerald Patterson's pioneering work in this area[13] for more information, and the same principles apply to classrooms).[14] In

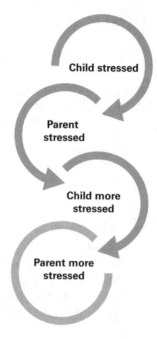

Figure 6.1. The negative cycle.

contrast, research shows that praising children or making positive statements at least four times more often than giving commands or reprimands is effective at reducing behavioral problems
and improving social skills.

No one can be positive all of the time. However, if you work
on being positive and building new skills, it will make you and
the child happier. Being positive works to increase more of the
behaviors that you want and decrease the behaviors you don't
want. You will be amazed at how much more you can get a child
to do (willingly) if you keep it positive!

HOW TO KEEP IT POSITIVE

*Praise a child four times more often than you give commands or cor-
rections.* Recognize how hard he or she is working to live in a
neurotypical world. Be sure to celebrate every effort and sign of
progress, rather than only praising success. Every day, praise
four times more often than you give commands and reprimands
(Figure 6.2). If you can make the ratio 5:1 of praise to command

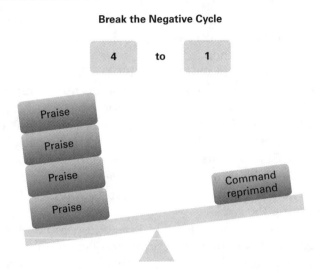

Break the Negative Cycle

4 to 1

Praise

Praise

Praise

Praise

Command reprimand

Figure 6.2. Use a 4:1 ratio (or greater) of praise to reprimands.

or reprimand, even better![15] Keeping to this ratio also trains you to pay more attention to the things that are going well than to things that need improvement. Use praise to motivate your child or student (or spouse, sister, boss) to do things that are hard. Try to avoid giving vague praise (e.g., "You are such a good girl") or praise that isn't true (e.g., "You are the smartest kid in the world!"). The praise should be specific and true, or the child will quickly learn to disregard it. Specific and true praise is often based on observations of the effort needed to achieve something rather than on successful completion. Be sure to validate what the child is experiencing and his or her efforts to be more flexible and organized. Some examples of specific and true praise include the following:

- "That's a very creative thought!"
- "I see that you're really stuck and you're working hard to be flexible."
- "I liked the way you solved that problem on you own."
- "You worked really hard on that puzzle."
- "I'm so proud of you for working hard on that!"

Hugs, high fives, thumbs up, and rewards on the child's point system also count as praise, as long as the child knows what you mean when you use them.

This is easiest to practice at a time of calm (e.g., not rushing for the school bus). Try sticking to this ratio for 1 hour with the child and watch what happens. You want to strive to keep to this overall ratio, but it doesn't have to apply moment to moment. For example, if your child is trying to paint your pet cat pink, you don't have to first say, "I really like that color pink. You are so creative! You are holding that paintbrush very well. Great job being careful to get as much paint on the cat as you can" to balance "Stop painting the cat!"

You can also improve your praise-to-command ratio by reducing your commands or reprimands (see number 8 in this subsection for more information on how to pick your battles). You can also reduce your commands by using the Socratic method. See Find a Hero in this subsection and the Why Think "Can't, Not Won't" subsection of Problem 7 later in this chapter. The following are some examples of reducing commands:

- Instead of saying, "Get your shoes on," ask "What else do you need to get ready to leave?" or you can prompt by saying, "I have my shoes and coat on, I am ready to go."

- Instead of commanding, "Finish your work," ask (in a pleasant voice) "What are you supposed to be doing now?"

Build on the child's strengths to increase his or her self-esteem and help him or her to learn new things and to better use new skills. Start with those skills that are most important to the child. Common strengths of children with ASD include memorizing, noticing details, thinking logically, visualizing problems and understanding visual information, maintaining focus on interesting activities, following clear rules, and behaving with honesty and integrity. Make a list of the child's strengths and hang it on the fridge, or make a note of it in the child's school or therapy file. Make a list of your own strengths, too.

Don't say don't: Telling someone what to do and recognizing their efforts is more powerful than telling someone what not to do. An easy way to remember this is "Don't say don't." If you see someone who is running and is about to fall into a huge pothole, it is more helpful to shout "Stop!" than to shout "Don't fall into that hole!" Try to focus most on what you want the child to do: say "Can you teach your brother to play Go Fish?" instead of saying "Don't run around the house like a bronco!"

Expect more, get more; expect less, get less. Have high expectations. Of course, expecting more than a child can realistically give can leave you both feeling frustrated and discouraged. You want to hold your expectations one step higher than what the child is currently doing in order to keep him or her making consistent progress. Parents and the professionals who are working with the child should hold similarly high standards.

TIP

Motivation

The internal motivation that works for you or other children won't work the same way for those with autism spectrum disorder (ASD), because those rewards aren't always logical or explicit. When we asked children with ASD what could help them learn new skills, the universal reply was "give us rewards!" One insightful 13 year old, Peter Berg, said, "When something is difficult or unexpected, somehow getting bonus points helps me reset my brain. Without points, I can't do it, even if I want to."

Develop a reward system. Change is hard for any of us, and most of us do better at working toward a big goal if there is a reward at the end, whether it is a chocolate after an unpleasant task or a new outfit when we lose weight. However, rewards are particularly important for children with ASD. ASD has a profound effect on children's internal motivational systems: children with ASD may be motivated by the things in which they are interested but unable to be motivated to do the things you or other adults are interested in having them do just because you want them to do them. In other words, a child with ASD is self-directed in motivation and attention. When you want the child to learn something new, especially something that does not come naturally, be sure you are offering a tangible, meaningful reward. When a skill is new, reward the child for each step he or she is able to perform. As his or her skills grow and develop, you should reward the ability to perform them independently. By rewarding this independence, you are ultimately increasing the child's independence and fostering confidence to problem-solve independently. Integrate a point system into the daily routine that rewards expected behavior. Make this reward system as simple, clear, and flexible as possible (see Putting It into Action: Setting Up a Reward System later in this section). The easier it is to use and understand, the more likely you will be to use it. The more you use it, the more powerful the system becomes.

- *Use visuals:* Points should be awarded in a visual, systematic way, such as on a chart or with a tangible reward, and counted frequently throughout the day.

- *Daily rewards:* Points should be redeemed frequently for something the child finds highly motivating (e.g., computer time). Extra points can be banked over time for a larger item.

- *Bonus points:* Extra, unexpected points or rewards should be given for extra effort. Intermittent reinforcement is the most powerful kind of reinforcement. This is why slot machines work, or why a surprise $20 gift card for a job well done is more powerful than a $20 raise. Give bonus points for helping a sibling, classmate, or friend; handling the unexpected; or any other positive behavior you want to encourage.

- *Avoid taking away points:* Rewards and praise are much more effective than punishment for those with ASD (punishment can set off a new cycle of inflexibility, which can actually make things worse).

- *Rewards aren't the same thing as bribes:* A bribe comes before the action (I pay you to vote a certain way on legislation tomorrow). A reward comes after the action (like your paycheck).

Find a hero. Help the child find a personal hero and set goals to be more like that hero. The hero may be a historical or literary figure, a cartoon character, someone the child knows, or someone famous. You might want to find a personal hero for yourself, too. Together, you can each explore your hero's meaning. Was there a time when the hero had to be flexible? A time when the hero had to accomplish something hard? How about a time when the hero had to resist distraction (a whim) and focus on a bigger picture (target) goal? After this discussion, you can use references to the hero to build new skills (e.g., "What would Amelia Earhart do in this situation?").

Nurture your sense of humor. Surround yourself with people who can help you laugh or have fun. Watch comedies. Laugh at yourself. Make jokes. Be silly together. Try to have as much fun as you can. Humor is particularly effective in getting around inflexibility with children and teens with ASD, so try some of the How to Make It Fun suggestions in Chapters 3, 4, and 5.

Pick your battles. You can't fight effectively on all fronts without a massive army. This may be one of the most often recommended strategies, and yet it can be the most difficult to use every day. There may be so many areas that need improvement, but a child will not make progress if you try to tackle too many at once. If you try to teach everything at once, you will end up exhausted, frustrated, and ineffective, and the child will feel overwhelmed. Work on only a couple of skills at a time, not more. Start with two goals: one that you think is going to be pretty easy (e.g., "remember to brush your teeth before bed" or "put your homework in the homework bin when I ask for it"), to ensure early success, and one that will make the biggest difference (e.g., "take turns with your brother," "let your classmates finish talking before you start talking," or "start your work on your own"). Include these goals in the reward system, and then ignore everything else that you can. This will help shift everyone to a more positive, skill-building environment. That means that if using a napkin at dinner isn't a current "battle," you ignore the food on your child's face. Or, you can praise your other child for remembering to use a napkin.

Let's revisit Johnny, the 10 year old with ASD who missed the school bus in the example in Table 1.1. The school bus is coming in 10 minutes and he isn't quite ready—he's still eating his breakfast. Table 6.1 shows examples of how the morning looks when the parent keeps it negative, and again when the parent keeps it positive and uses the other suggestions in this book. Figure 6.3 summarizes the key strategies involved in keeping it positive.

Table 6.1. Examples of negative versus positive responses

	Keeping it negative (-)		Keeping it positive (+) or neutral (n)	
Parent	(Urgently) Hurry up and finish your breakfast.	-	(Calmly) The bus is coming in 10 minutes. I'm going to get your morning checklist for you.	n
Johnny	I'm still hungry.		I'm still hungry.	
Parent	You should have thought of that when you hit snooze on your alarm.	-	You can keep eating. Here is your checklist. What do you need to do next?	n
Johnny	I was tired! I hate mornings!	-	(Looks at list) Brush my teeth.	+
Parent	You haven't even brushed your teeth yet! You have to hurry up!	- -	Great. While you're brushing your teeth, I'll pack a (granola bar, hard-boiled egg, cheese stick, toast) for you to eat on the bus.	+
Johnny	I don't want to go to school.	-	(Goes to brush teeth. Brushes teeth, and then gets distracted making faces in the mirror.)	+ -
Parent	I am sick of you missing the bus, and then I have to drive and wait in the long dropoff line and you're late for school. So hurry up!	- -	What's next on your checklist?	n
Johnny	(Feeling overloaded) No!	-	Shoes, then backpack.	+
Parent	Where are your shoes? Why do we have to search the house every day for your shoes?	-	Yes! Do you know where they are?	+
Johnny	(Stomps around, slowly, looking for shoes.)	-	By the front door.	+
Parent	The bus is here! Run!	- -	Woo-hoo! Right where they should be! Good thinking, getting them ready last night. You have 5 minutes until bus time.	+ + -
Johnny	(Runs out of the house, anxious about missing the bus and being late to school. Leaves homework on the dining room table. Didn't brush his teeth or finish breakfast.)	- - - -	(Puts on shoes and backpack.)	+ +
Parent	(Feels frustrated. Tries to decide whether to take the homework to school.)	-	Hey, I think you are going to beat the neighbors to the bus stop. You are *so* on target this morning! That's 15 extra minutes of computer time for being ready in time.	+ + +

Remembering to Keep It Positive

4:1 ratio of praise to command or reprimand

Build on child's strengths.

Don't say "don't."

Expect more, get more.

Use a reward system.

Who is the child's hero?

Keep your sense of humor.

Pick your battles.

Figure 6.3. Visual: Remembering to Keep It Positive.

PUTTING IT INTO ACTION
Setting Up a Reward System

If the Child Needs a Concrete or Tangible Reminder

Create a marble jar reward system. This is an easy-to-implement and flexible system:

1. Find a clear jar or plastic container, or you can use a clear bag. Put the child's name on it, or he or she may want to decorate the container. You can put a sign on the jar reminding him or her about the thing that will earn rewards.
2. Choose an easy item to drop in the jar. You could use coins, poker chips, pieces of pasta, glass beads or marbles, or even home-made "bonus bucks" or tickets.
3. Assign values to the reward, such as each marble equals 1 minute of computer or television or game time, or can be used toward a purchase (e.g., iTunes, books). You should come up with the rewards together, and the child should be able to earn the rewards pretty quickly to start with.
4. Every time you catch the child being good or trying hard, drop one to five marbles into the container. Be sure to tell him or her exactly how that reward was earned (e.g., "Great job doing your homework. That's two marbles!" or "Well done waiting your turn in line today! That's two marbles."). When you are away from the container, you can carry a zippered plastic bag to hold the rewards as the child earns them.
5. Assign a higher value or give more marbles when situations or skills are particularly difficult (e.g., "You were right on time this morning and earned five marbles!" or "You completed the paragraph all on your own and earned five marbles!").
6. Give bonus rewards for particularly good behaviors (e.g., "You did a great job turning that big deal into a littler deal. You earned 10 bonus marbles!"). Try to give bonus rewards every day.
7. Share this system with school personnel, grandparents, therapists, and anyone who could use it while they are with the child.

If the Child Doesn't Need a Tangible Reminder

Design a point or check system like that shown in Figure 6.4.

J's jobs:	Sun.	Mon.	Tues.	Weds.	Thurs.	Fri.	Sat.
Clearing the table	✓✓✓		✓	✓		✓	✓✓
Using polite words	✓		✓✓✓		✓	✓✓✓	
Getting into bed by 9 p.m.	✓	✓		✓		✓	✓
Bonus points	✓✓✓		✓		✓✓		✓
Total points earned	8	1	5	2	3	5	4
Each check = 5 extra minutes of computer time. Total computer time earned today.	40	5	25	10	15	25	20
Computer minutes used (including carryover)	25	20	25	0	20	30	20
Carryover minutes	15	0	0	10	5	0	0

Figure 6.4. Example of a check system for rewards.

Problem 2: *Child is too overwhelmed to learn a new skill or to behave appropriately*

Solution: *Avoid overload*

WHY AVOID OVERLOAD?

Remember the last time you felt completely overwhelmed? Maybe you were rushing out the door to get your child to an appointment, the phone started ringing, you realized you had forgotten an important errand, and your teenager started whining about needing to get to the mall, at which point all you wanted to do was crawl back into bed and take a nap. These are the times when we are most likely to yell, injure ourselves, or make mistakes. All of us have a breaking point at which we feel overloaded and unable to listen well, problem-solve, or control our emotions or behaviors. Reaching that point is never useful. It reduces our effectiveness, and it leads us to do and say things that make us feel bad about ourselves.

Children with ASD are more easily overloaded than others, because their brains are best suited for dealing with information one predictable detail at a time. They can get overloaded when they have to manage too much information at once, or when they have to respond to changing, unpredictable situations. For people with ASD, biologically based inflexibility makes any new social situation or a change of plans especially overloading. Once overloaded, they often can't handle information that they can easily understand at other times. They also can lose behavioral control, becoming more repetitive, anxious, impulsive, inattentive, or even aggressive.

HOW TO AVOID OVERLOAD

Predict overload. Know what overloads the child. Different children are overloaded by different situations or demands. Some are overloaded by language, others by noisy children. Some children are very easily overloaded if they are even a little bit hungry, whereas others are overwhelmed by any uncertainty in their day. You cannot avoid all sources of overload, but you should also feel comfortable taking reasonable steps to buffer the child from specific situations or demands that are especially hard for him or her to manage.

 Don't add the straw that breaks the camel's back. Know what signs warn of overload. Children have different ways of showing that they are starting to feel overloaded. Some act more impulsively, others are more repetitive, others simply withdraw. Many children give physical signs of overload, such as tensing their body or clenching their fists. Make sure you know what signs the child makes so that you can respond before he or she is completely overloaded.

Make things as predictable as possible. One of the best ways to avoid overload is to make things as predictable as possible. See the subsection Putting It into Action: The Activity Companion later in this section.

- *Let the child make as many choices as possible.* If he or she feels control over plans and daily schedules, he or she will be more invested and feel things are more under control and predictable. This does not mean that you turn over control in all situations, but rather that you provide choices as often as possible. For example, you can offer two choices for a snack, choices for the order in which he or she completes assignments, or choices for the topic of a writing assignment.

- *Provide explicit assurance that certain routines will remain unchanged.* Self-soothing routines (e.g., watching the same video every day after school, sitting in the same seat in the classroom, visiting the same counselor or special educator before school starts each day, pacing alone in another room, reading at a certain time each day) that are not otherwise harmful should be respected, as long as they do not interfere with essential social engagement or work completion. If children with ASD can maintain some of these routines, they can better handle change in other areas.

- Establish regular routines for after school, at bedtime, and at other times (see solution to Problem 3: Break It Down).

Preview for the child when entering any new situation, reviewing the specific things that he or she can expect to happen—but do not promise anything of which you are unsure. Help the child prepare for things that you cannot predict or be certain about. Ask questions such as "Is there a chance that we might sit in the back of the theater? Is there a chance that we might have to sit in the front?" or "Is there a chance that the substitute won't know our special sign for when you need a break?" These questions will prepare the child for those things that you can't control, and also help you and the child come up with Plan B's that the child can implement if needed.

Structure nonroutine, chaotic, or large-group events with a specific schedule, plan, or job. Make a checklist of expected events on a family trip, field trip, or any unusual activity. Also preview possible problems that might come up and how you will manage them. Consider this example of Cousin Mark's wedding:

- *Preview and predict as much of the event as you can.* "We are going to Cousin Mark's wedding this afternoon. Lots of different things will happen there. Some might be boring. Some will be fun. First we will sit in the church and there will be music, and the people at the front of the church will talk. Then we will go to a big party where there will be lots of good food to eat. I do not know exactly when they will serve the food. There will probably be music and some people will dance. Your aunts and uncles and cousins will be there, and they will want to talk to you and play with you. Sometimes wedding parties are loud. If you think it is too loud at the party, you should come and tell me so we can make a plan for taking a break. If I think it is time to take a break I will come and find you. By 9 o'clock it will be time for us to go home."

- *Provide one or two specific rules that the child should follow.* "During the ceremony in church, you will have to sit still and be quiet. What should be our sign to each other if we need to remember to be quiet in the church? Would you like to take a book to the church to help you stay quiet?"

- *Give the child a visual, such as a checklist or a map.* "Let's make a list of the different things we think will happen at the wedding, and you can check them off when they happen."

- *If possible, give the child a specific role or a job to do.* "Cousin Mark wants to have lots of pictures of the wedding party so he can remember it. I need you to help him by taking pictures of the party with your camera."

- *Predict potential problems: what could go wrong?* "What if you don't like the cake? What if you need to go to the bathroom while we're sitting in the church? What if you don't like the music? What is the most important goal of this event?"

Expect field trips, assemblies, holidays, and vacations to be difficult. Because these times involve disruptions to the routine, you may need to spend extra time preparing the child for them. It may be useful to provide a schedule, explicitly reviewing what things will be like normal (e.g., he or she will still eat three meals a day and go to bed at night, you will still be with him or her all day) and what things might be different. Make sure everyone (including you) gets some downtime. You may want to consider a special reward for the child's successful participation in (or tolerance of) particularly challenging events. Let him or her know in advance that work will be rewarded and identify that reward, perhaps even giving a choice between favorite rewards.

- *Regularly schedule downtime when the child knows he or she can be alone or with one trusted adult doing an activity he or she enjoys.* You wouldn't ask children who are dyslexic to read all day long. Children who struggle with social and EF tasks similarly need breaks from people and demands. School is typically overloading to children with ASD. Downtime can be scheduled into the child's school day (e.g., the child can sit quietly in the resource room for 30 minutes and read, the child can eat lunch in a classroom) and also into after-school hours.

- *Spontaneously provide downtime when the child is becoming overwhelmed or stressed.* This can involve removing him or her from a specific activity (e.g., leave the large family reunion after 2 hours instead of staying for the whole evening, send the child to the resource room to deliver a note that says this child needs a break) or pulling him or her aside into a quiet place for a break.

Provide a buffer from or reduce stimulation and disorder if the child seems overwhelmed. Parents can create a safe haven in the home, and to a lesser extent teachers can do the same at school. If the child has sensory sensitivities in any of the following areas, try these suggestions:

- *Auditory:* Rugs, cork floors, and wall hangings can all make a room quieter. Tennis balls can be put on the bottom of chairs to reduce scraping noises. Experiment with turning off background noise (television, computer sound, or radios). Use white noise machines or fans to block out unavoidable and distressing noises. Earplugs and headphones can also be helpful.

- *Visual:* Aim for less cluttered surfaces and walls and consider whether bright or harsh lighting affects the child. Reducing fluorescent lighting or having the child wear a baseball cap or sunglasses can also reduce visual overload. Provide something pleasing to look at and focus on (e.g., favorite comic book, tablet computer) at overstimulating times. Place the child next to calm people and face him or her away from the most chaotic part of the room.

- *Olfactory (smell):* Some children with ASD are particularly sensitive to smell. Avoid using scented cleaning and/or body products (e.g., perfume, soaps). Some foods and gums can also be problematic.

- *Tactile (touch):* If the child is sensitive to the way things feel on the skin, you can remove tags from clothing and avoid tight socks, irritating waistbands, and other sources of discomfort. Some children with ASD are soothed by deep pressure and benefit from hugs or even weighted vests, whereas others like physical contact only if they can initiate it. Many children with ASD do not like to be touched, especially if they are not expecting it.

- *After-school hours can be especially important times to create a buffered home environment, because your child will be recovering from the overstimulating school environment.* If the dynamics of your family make creating such a haven for your entire house difficult, consider creating one space where your child can retreat after school (e.g., his own room, a tent over his or her bed).

Smaller is usually better. Expect a child's ability to control impulses, anxiety, or repetitive behaviors to decrease as the number of people or complexity of the group increases.

- *When in doubt, reduce the size of the group the child is in* (e.g., invite three children to the birthday party, not 12). Select times for outings based on when the crowd will be smallest (e.g., movie matinees, early-morning museum trips). Excuse the child from field trips, or bring a special person who can provide individual supports to the child. Sit with the child at assemblies.

- *Teach new skills in small groups.* For example, many children with ASD learn social skills best by first practicing new scripts (e.g., what to say when you want to play with someone) with one other person. Once they master a skill one to one, then they can try it out in a small group. You do not know if a child has completely mastered something until it is demonstrated in a larger group.

- *If the child is overloaded at school, seek opportunities for smaller groups* (e.g., many children with ASD benefit from eating lunch in a classroom with a teacher and several other children, as opposed to in a large cafeteria).

Request accommodations. Small things can make a big difference. All airlines will let families board at the early boarding time for passengers with disabilities; many amusement parks provide special passes for children with disabilities that allow them to avoid standing in line (Disney theme parks are famous for this). Some museums have sensory-friendly tours. There are so many times when having a child with ASD makes things more difficult. There is no reason why you shouldn't take the opportunity for a break when it exists. The child will be less stressed, and everyone will benefit.

PUTTING IT INTO ACTION
Predicting and Reducing Overload

The worksheet shown in Figure 6.5 can help with preventing overload.

PUTTING IT INTO ACTION
The Activity Companion

Use the worksheet shown in Figure 6.6 to help prepare for any activity.

Problem 3: *My child has trouble getting started with things or learning new skills.*

Solution: *Break it down.*

WHY BREAK THINGS DOWN (WHEN THIS CHILD IS SO SMART)?

Children with ASD have trouble identifying the main idea and integrating information. On the other hand, their command of details is often remarkable, and they tend to have excellent abilities to analyze and memorize small chunks of explicit information.[16]

This contradiction leads to a common problem: People may hear a child speak with a large vocabulary and provide a lot of factual information, leading them to assume that he or she can handle all kinds of information. They assume that the child should be able to handle writing an essay, or taking good notes on a lecture, or packing up for school dismissal all on his or her own.

Predicting and Reducing Overload

Catch Overload Early

Remember the last time the child became overloaded. What occurred 15, 10, and 5 minutes before overload? Were there any warning signs? List overload warning signs he or she makes (e.g., starts to talk louder or faster or in a higher voice, gets stuck on something, hums, increases repetitive behaviors, becomes more impulsive, becomes more anxious, starts refusing to do things, clenches body):

1. _____

2. _____

List triggers that lead to overload (e.g., hunger, crowds, fatigue, too much talking, writing):

1. _____

2. _____

Defuse the Situation: What to Do

Remember the last time you were able to help the child avoid overload. What did you do that calmed him or her (e.g., steer to a quiet place, touch him or her, make a sign that cued him or her to calm down, use other visual cues, leave him or her alone)?

1. _____

2. _____

Figure 6.5. Predicting and Reducing Overload worksheet.   *(continued)*

Figure 6.5. *(continued)* (page 2 of 2)

What coping strategies did the child use effectively (e.g., take deep breaths, distract self with a favorite activity, think of a favorite thing or place, ask for a hug)?

1. _____

2. _____

What did you do that helped you stay calm (e.g., breathe deeply, think of how much you love your child, think of a calming melody, look at the child and put yourself in his or her shoes)?

1. _____

2. _____

Defuse the Situation: What *Not* to Do

Once a child is overloaded, it is usually *not* helpful to:

1. *Talk.* Reasoning at this stage makes things worse. The child is unlikely to be able to process what is said. Learning cannot happen when a child is overloaded.

2. *Act impulsively.* If you don't know how to help, don't do anything. An escalation of your emotions will probably escalate the child.

3. *Rush.* It can take a long time to recover from overload. Some children need hours of downtime.

An experienced emergency room doctor training new doctors once said, "Don't just do something, stand there!" When things are not going well, it is hard for most of us to hold back, but that is how we observe what is happening and avoid making things worse than they already are.

The Activity Companion

Where are we going?

How will we get there?

Who will be there?

What will we see and do?

What is our goal?

What is our schedule?

What are the rules?

What could go wrong?

Do we have a Plan B?

Figure 6.6. The Activity Companion worksheet.

However, the latter type of activity requires organization and integration of information and management of multiple steps, skills that are especially hard for people with ASD. In a research study, we found that every time we compared a simple task to the same task with added information or steps (e.g., copy a triangle versus copy a triangle within a triangle within a square), children with ASD did much worse on the task with more information or steps.[17] Of course, complexity is harder for everyone, but the children in our study did much worse than typical children on the complicated tasks, whereas they did as well as or better than typical children on the simple tasks. By breaking down tasks, we play to the strengths of most children with ASD, but by failing to break down tasks we can make them look much less able than they really are.

HOW TO BREAK THINGS DOWN AND HELP A CHILD BUILD UP TO MASTERING NEW SKILLS

Break any task that is hard for the child into progressively smaller chunks until he or she is successful. Examples:

- If the child struggles to answer open-ended questions such as "How was school today?" ask specific questions such as "What did you eat today at lunch?"

- If the child starts protesting when you tell him to clean up his or her room or just wanders off in a daze, ask him or her to put all of the dirty clothes in the hamper and then come back to you for the next assignment. As he or she completes each of these small steps and reports back to you, reward him or her with specific praise and perhaps a bonus point or the equivalent in your reinforcement system.

- If the child takes one look at a page of math problems and says he or she can't do the work, cover up all the problems but one with a blank piece of paper.

- If the child keeps putting off a report for school, tell him or her to find one source of information on the topic and then show you what he or she found, or set a timer and have him or her work on the task for 10 minutes and then take a break.

The three R's of multistep tasks: Recipes, Rules, and Routines. It is also important to spell out the steps and rules of multistep tasks.

Would you watch a chef make a complicated meal on television and then attempt to cook it later without a recipe? Children will be helped by having a checklist or a recipe, and most complex tasks can be organized and presented in written recipe or checklist format. You will find that the trouble you take to write down steps is usually more than made up for by the reduction in the amount of time you will have to spend nagging and reminding. In other situations, specific rules that are written down are most helpful and can take the pressure off you to always be stating and enforcing rules. Examples include the following:

- A whiteboard or laminated checklist in the child's folder that lists the steps for doing long division, writing a complete paragraph, packing up at the end of school, and other frequent tasks, each with a box to check off next to it

- A paper checklist on a clipboard for getting ready to go to school each morning (see Putting It into Action: Making a Morning Checklist).

- A "homework routine" that pops up on the child's laptop or constitutes a special section of his or her notebook, specifying all the steps to follow, from writing down an assignment to putting the books in the backpack

- A "how to write a paper checklist" that starts with brainstorming the topic and goes through spell-checking the document

- If the visual presentation of many steps on a checklist is overwhelming, use a small flip chart. Each step is presented on a separate index card, and they can be connected by a ring.

- Three rules for a fun playdate (e.g., the guest gets to pick the first activity) can be printed on an index card that is reviewed right before the playmate arrives.

- Rules for computer time (e.g., obey time limits, no Internet) can be posted next to the computer.

Figure out what parts of a task are most difficult for the child. When a child is struggling to complete a task, the first step is to analyze the components of the task so that you can understand what is going wrong and intervene in that area.

Remember to provide just the right amount of support; not too much, not too little. This point was discussed in Chapter 2, but providing the wrong amount of support is a common mistake and warrants another reminder.

Explicitly help decode or break down new or complex material.

- *If the child has trouble successfully joining others* at a playground, sit down together on a bench before letting him or her play. Talk about what you see. Who is playing games that the child likes; are there children on the playground who are especially fun to play with or who have been mean in the past?

- *If the child is being rude to other students in class,* find a quiet time to talk with the child about what specific behaviors are hurting the classmate's feelings and what alternative things the child can do when feeling frustrated with classmates.

- *Help the child make connections to previously learned material.* If a child is struggling to learn new material at school, try to relate it to other ideas or concepts he or she already understands, or put new information in a familiar context (e.g., "This percentage math problem reminds me of those pie fraction problems you had last week.").

PUTTING IT INTO ACTION
Making a Morning Checklist

Figure 6.7 shows a sample checklist that could be used for morning routines.

Problem 4: *The child won't listen to me or follow directions.*

Solution: *Talk less, write more.*

WHY TALK LESS, WRITE MORE (WHEN THIS CHILD HAS A BIGGER VOCABULARY THAN I DO)?

Children with ASD need to see visuals and hear consistent, streamlined language to learn new skills, carry out routines,

Morning Checklist		
8:00	✓	Turn off alarm clock.
	✓	Get out of bed.
		Go to the bathroom.
8:05	✓	Eat breakfast.
8:20		Take off PJs, put on clothes:
		Underwear
		Pants
		Shirt
		Socks
		Shoes
8:30		Brush teeth.
8:35		Put on coat.
8:40		Leave for bus.

Figure 6.7.   Sample morning checklist.

and problem-solve. In contrast, think about the last time you put together a piece of furniture or built a model with LEGOs. If you are like most people, you probably silently (or not so silently) talked yourself through at least some of the steps. Typical children do the same thing. They can use the words someone has spoken, words they have read, or their own words to guide their behavior.[18,19] They talk themselves through a math problem or packing up school materials at the end of the day. This "self-talk" is a tool for planning and organizing actions. It gives us access to things we have learned from previous experience or have been told. In this way, we can remember our plans and goals, as well as the rules and the steps needed to achieve them. Studies show that self-talk does not work well for many children with ASDs.[20–23] Even when they have big vocabularies and good basic language skills, they do better with visual supports. Thus, a child with ASD may be least successful when having to listen to your words and act on them without benefit of visual supports or memorized simple phrases.

HOW TO TALK LESS, WRITE MORE

Streamline your language. Use as few words as possible, as consistently as possible, to help the child remember specific things he or she has been taught about how best to manage his or her behavior in demanding situations. This book helps you teach consistent language to talk about being flexible and staying focused on goals. You have learned key words such as *flexibility,* and short scripts such as *"Is this a big deal or a little deal?"* In order to leverage this learning at times when the child is stressed by unexpected events or demands to think creatively and flexibly, it will be essential that the child's parents, teachers, and therapists use the same words and phrases consistently. The child will depend on those specific words to trigger understanding of the situation. Imagine that your student just found out that he forgot to bring in the Pokemon cards that he wanted to show you for free time. His face is becoming tense, and he looks like he is about to either cry or yell. How might you respond? Examples are shown in Table 6.2.

Provide a visual. We provided you with ideas for visuals to help build new EF skills, but you can also use these techniques if a child is having trouble following a multiple-step procedure or doing something independently (e.g., putting his or her name on papers, turning lights off when leaving room, flushing the toilet). Experiment with giving him or her a reminder, such as a picture, written checklist, or other visual reminder. For example, you could put a sticky note on the bathroom mirror or next to the toilet paper or faucet that says, "Flush!" or use a whiteboard on which you write each action needed to complete a school assignment.

Don't say it, write it. Some children with ASD respond much better to written than oral requests. Again, whiteboards are very

Table 6.2.   Examples of talking less, using the key words and scripts

Instead of saying . . .	Say . . .
"I knew this would happen when we didn't write a note to your mom. Don't get upset about this. Just calm down."	"That makes me feel frustrated, too. We will have to be flexible."
"Okay, so we can't look at your cards for free time. I will help you find something else we can do. I wonder if we could go take a walk, or maybe we should play a game."	"Our Plan A didn't work. Let's make a Plan B."
"Don't act like this is the end of the world. You can just show me the cards next time. It's not like the whole day is ruined" or "I know this feels like a big deal, but it isn't."	"Is this a big deal or a little deal?" (Pause to listen to answer.) "How can we make it into a little deal?"

helpful. If a child reacts badly when you ask him or her to do something and you find yourself getting swept into an escalating power struggle, try writing your question or request on a whiteboard and handing it to him or her with a marker. Many times, you will get a much more constructive response that way.

Use flowcharts. Another technique that can be especially effective is a flowchart that allows a child to replay a problematic scenario and then rewrite it the way he or she wishes it had gone. Built into these flowcharts is a logical progression that visually demonstrates that the problem scenario did not result in the outcome the child wanted. An example of a flowchart is shown in Figure 6.8.

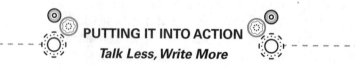

PUTTING IT INTO ACTION
Talk Less, Write More

Get and set up whiteboards for the rooms at home, classrooms at school, and therapist's office.

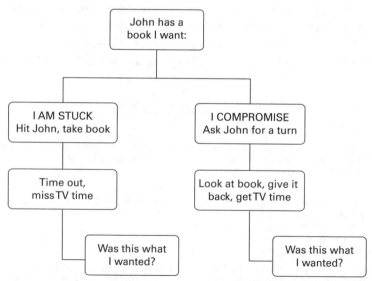

Figure 6.8. Example of a flowchart as a visual support. (From Cannon, L., Kenworthy, L., Alexander, K.C., Werner, M.A., & Anthony, L.G. [2011]. *Unstuck and on target!: An executive function curriculum to improve flexibility for children with autism spectrum disorders, research edition* [p. 72]. Baltimore, MD: Paul H. Brookes Publishing Co.; adapted by permission.)

Problem 5: *Sometimes I feel overloaded or am inflexible myself.*

Solution: *Put on your own oxygen mask first, so you can model flexibility for the child.*

WHY SHOULD I TAKE CARE OF MYSELF (WHEN IT'S MY CHILD WHO IS HAVING DIFFICULTY)?

Parenting, teaching, or working therapeutically with children can be both rewarding and stressful. Research studies have shown that parenting a child with an ASD can be highly stressful and require even larger accommodations in a parent's life.[24,25] Although the effects on teachers haven't been studied as extensively, it also stands to reason that teachers, who are increasingly being asked to work with children with developmental disabilities in inclusive classroom settings without much support, also experience stress and are overwhelmed at times.

Remember the last time you flew, and the flight attendants instructed that, if there is a loss of cabin pressure, you should put on your oxygen mask first and then help others? They tell you this because you need to be able to breathe in order to effectively help a child, and you are also modeling for the child how to take care of oneself. If you are a parent, remember that every member of your family needs as much love and support as your child with an ASD. Do things that are just for you, and encourage your other family members to do the same. Reward yourself for doing things that are hard, too! Regardless of your role in the child's life, remember that you are best able to support his or her learning when you have the energy to model good problem solving, flexible thinking, and goal-oriented behavior yourself.

KEEP YOUR "FREEZER" WELL-STOCKED

Mother and author Brenda Boyd recommends the "freezer tip": just as you regularly restock your freezer so you always have something on hand, you also need to pay attention to your own needs so that you are more patient and resilient during the inevitable times when parenting is a challenge.[26]

HOW TO TAKE CARE OF YOURSELF

Create a circle of support. Many of the specific suggestions in this section are most relevant to parents, but the general principle that the child's teacher and therapists also need supports is important. If you work with a child with ASD, make sure you have a colleague who also understands the disorder with whom you can discuss the child, as there may be times when he or she confuses or frustrates you. Ask for help often, from many people. Make a list of "go-to" people whom you can trust to keep the child's best interests in mind and who can be counted on to show they believe that he or she is a great kid, even when he or she messes up. You may want to formally ask these people to be a member of the child's circle of support. More people are willing to help than you may realize, but you have to ask. Try to make requests as specific as possible. It is even okay to ask strangers for help. The next time your child has a meltdown in public, turn to the person shooting you dirty looks and use a script such as "My child has autism (or a brain disorder, or whatever label you feel comfortable with) and we are just going to have to wait until this storm passes. Can you see if you can get her (or me) a drink of water? It really helps." Some parents carry cards that explain autism and hand them out to "curious" passersby, making the tantrum a teaching opportunity. Most people have the capacity for empathy when it is explicitly requested.

Build a treatment team that addresses the child's needs and provides you with validation and support. This can take time and some comparison shopping on your part; at a minimum, the child's school professionals, medical doctors, psychologists, speech and language pathologists, occupational therapists, or other caregivers should consistently include parents in the treatment process, recognize the child's strengths, respect the family, communicate with each other, target problems that the child and parents think are important, and contribute to positive changes in the child's behavior and skill development.

Parent as a team, too. Often one parent not only takes the primary responsibility for the daily work but also is the one who becomes educated about ASD. That parent then increasingly speaks a language the other parent or caregivers do not. This in turn increases the burden on that parent and distances him or her both from the child and from the co-parent. When both parents are involved as much as possible, however, communication is easier, and each parent is more able to bring unique contributions to the child's development.

Share your feelings and experiences. Find someone (e.g., partner, friend, family, spiritual leader, doctor) to talk to about your feelings. Many parents also find support groups helpful, and teachers often form their own informal support groups. If support groups aren't for you, consider joining an online network. It often helps to know that someone else shares in your challenges and triumphs, and other teachers and parents can be a wealth of practical knowledge. Research tells us that any social network is a powerful force in improving one's overall sense of well-being and ability to cope, so it is also helpful to find a group that congregates around a shared interest (e.g., hobby, exercise, getting outdoors, religion or spirituality).

Nurture your other loved ones. Most parents who have a child with an ASD feel strain in their other close relationships. Often, partners have different emotional reactions to their child's diagnosis, have difficulty sharing their feelings, disagree on how to proceed with evaluations and interventions, and experience stressful financial and time constraints. Communicate, protect your time together, and try to avoid judging each other. Try to spend a little special time with your other children or family members.

Divide and conquer. Whole-family or whole-classroom activities can be enjoyable and fun, but they can also be stressful. It's okay for one parent or teacher to take the child with ASD and the other to take the other kids. Parents and teachers of children with ASD often find themselves heading in two different directions during leisure time. Trade places next time.

Parents, give yourselves downtime.

- Investigate respite services in your area. Respite care provides in-home or center-based care so you can have time to yourself or time to spend with other family members. If you cannot find respite care in your area, you can also train and hire someone yourself. See Putting It into Action: Finding Respite Care later in this section.

- Explore specialized camps for children with ASD, or look for a family camp that is designed for entire families that include a child with ASD.

Some parents have to be creative to fit in time each week for activities that will recharge them. Could you find another parent of a child with special needs and trade off babysitting? Could you sign up for an exercise class or volunteer at the local animal shelter while the child is in school? Arrange a weekly breakfast or lunch date with your spouse or partner during school hours?

Does your child with ASD remind you of someone? Accepting your child's challenges may involve addressing your own or your loved ones' difficulties. ASD traits—including social reticence, visual thinking, strongly focused interests, and pleasure in routines—tend to cluster in families. Often, a child's diagnosis leads family members to understand themselves and each other in new and empowering ways. This can increase tolerance and strengthen relationships, but it can also lead parents to be more frustrated or irritated with their own or their partner's traits. Don't feel guilty if you believe your child has inherited your or your partner's weaknesses. Your child has also inherited many of your strengths, which you are building on by seeking out evaluations and interventions.

PUTTING IT INTO ACTION
Finding Respite Care

Most families hire babysitters; families of children with ASD not only have greater need but require especially skillful care providers. Here are some suggestions for respite care:

- *Hire special help.* Advice from an experienced parent: "I've had really good success finding college and graduate students who are interested in doing in-home care. I've advertised on Craig's List, and I've also had some success using electronic bulletin boards at area universities. Connecting directly with programs in education, special education, and psychology would be another way. When things were really hard in our household, I hired two or even three such students and had our behavior consultant train them. They then worked in the house with parents at home for a period of time before we contemplated leaving them alone." A sample ad for babysitters is shown in Figure 6.9.

- *Look for free respite.* Check with your state or county organizations, nonprofits such as The Arc, autism waiver services, and religious organizations. Many provide grants or free or reduced-cost respite care. Some high school students need community service learning hours, as do Boy Scouts, and could be willing to

Seeking graduate student or mature undergrad to work from 4 to 8 p.m., two weekdays, supervising very bright and highly verbal 9-year-old boy with autism spectrum disorder. Interest or experience in psychology or special education a plus, and applied behavioral analysis training preferred. Must be engaging, creative, fun to be with, unflaggingly upbeat and positive, strong, and self-confident. Training from professional therapists will be provided. Candidate will eat dinner with the family and supervise afternoon/evening activities including play, homework, and bath. Internship credit possible.

Compensation: Market Rate

Figure 6.9. Sample ad seeking respite care.

provide some help for free. University organizations may also have student groups who are willing to partner with community groups looking for respite or other supports.

Problem 6: *Once the child gets stuck on something or overloaded, it takes a long time to get unstuck.*

Solution: *Have coping strategies ready.*

WHY HAVE COPING STRATEGIES READY?

Everyday life is often stressful for children with ASD. It is hard for them to be flexible, deal with social situations, and understand and manage their own feelings. For many children with ASD, even the sights and sounds of everyday life at its usual pace can be overloading. They may misunderstand a situation and/or focus on the negative aspects, getting worked up quickly. When a child with ASD is getting stuck or overloaded, he or she may not be aware of the buildup of feeling until it is too late to avoid a meltdown. Therefore, it is essential to teach simple coping strategies to help children with ASD become aware of their feelings and calm them. This will make your life and the child's life less stressful and create more time when the child is receptive to learning.

HOW TO HAVE COPING STRATEGIES READY

Use a visual rating system for identifying and changing feelings. Visual rating scales are very helpful for many children with ASD, and

- -

they can be particularly helpful to quantify abstract ideas such as feelings. A child's feelings can be represented visually as a thermometer, speedometer, number line, or other device; the representations all allow a child to rate how they are feeling with a visual tool. The purpose of the thermometer is twofold: 1) it will help the child better identify what he or she is feeling, and 2) the child will better be able to change how he or she is feeling by changing his or her thoughts or behaviors (e.g., "Am I bored? Maybe I should try to think of something fun to do." "Am I angry? Maybe I should try to calm down."). You can also use the thermometer yourself to show the child how it works (e.g., "I am feeling pretty frustrated by this traffic. I think I'm a 7 on the thermometer now. Can you help me calm down by playing I Spy with me?"). The representations work best if you use them to check in with the child on a regular basis, at times when he or she is feeling good and feeling neutral as well as when he or she is struggling. When the child is struggling, the ratings can be paired with a coping strategy that works (e.g., taking three deep breaths, thinking about a favorite place, taking a break). See Putting It into Action: Feelings Thermometer later in this section.

   Coping strategies. Help the child develop a short list of strategies for calming down. You may want to use the Putting It into Action: Coping Strategies Experiment (later in this section) to help the child discover which techniques will work best through experimentation. Prepare a variety of strategies useful in different situations (e.g., in the car, at the store, at recess, at a friend's house).

COPING STRATEGIES

Outside

- Run a lap
- Swing
- Bounce a ball

Take a Break

- Beanbag chair
- Head phones
- Soft pillow

_ _

Edible

- Get a drink of water
- Get juice
- Eat something chewy

Music

- Listening
- Humming

Other

- Reading
- Drawing
- Journaling
- Deep breathing
- Positive thoughts (e.g., beach)
- Bath and foot rub

_ _

Concrete reminders. For many children, a concrete reminder of the coping strategies can help.

- *Create a calming box:* Get a box and, with the child's help, assemble calming items or activities that can go in the box. Paper and markers, squish balls, action figures, LEGOs, and other small items may be useful. The calming box should be readily available when the child needs it. Activities that are humorous (e.g., Mad Libs, comics) may be helpful.

- *Coping cards:* Write, draw, or choose pictures to represent the coping strategies that the child selects. You may want to laminate the cards and attach them with a ring to make them easy for the child to flip through. Pictures of favorite activities or relaxing places may also act as calming reminders.

Incentives for using coping strategies: Reward the child for rating his or her feelings and for participating in developing coping strategies. At first, the child will require lots of structure and reminders to make use of coping strategies and will require specific incentives for doing so (e.g., you will earn five bonus points each time you use a coping strategy when you are too happy or

- -

too upset). The greatest rewards should occur when he or she is getting upset and effectively embraces a coping strategy before getting all the way to the end of the scale.

Movies, books, television, life: Daily life and media offer numerous opportunities to observe in people a variety of emotions: the upset child at the grocery store, the peaceful person floating in the pool, the sad woman in the movie. Make it a game with the child to "freeze frame" the movie or life moment and identify how the other person is feeling, using the visual rating system when you can. You can extend this to asking, "Why do you think he or she feels that way," and if the person is upset, "What can he or she do to feel better?"

Notice the peaceful or happy times. It is natural to think of coping when things are "hot" or stressful, but it is essential to point out the happy and peaceful times as well. Remember to ask children how they are feeling as much during the happy times as when they are upset. You want to avoid only associating the thermometer with feeling bad, and it's important for children to recognize good feelings, too. Usually it is best to practice strategies when a child is feeling calm.

Be a model of flexibility and calm. How can you teach flexibility if you are being rigid? There are times for parents, teachers, and other important adults to be flexible, too. When a child is getting upset, it is important for you to use your own coping strategies and keep a "clear mind" in order to help him or her (see Table 6.3). Remember, the child requires your clear and calm cue in order to use a coping strategy. If everyone "loses it," the coping strategies will be forgotten. The process of building the habit of using coping strategies takes persistence and patience. Realize that the first several attempts to move from bad feelings to effective coping will be difficult. Also remember that sometimes a child's emotions may get so intense that you need to, as the emergency room doctor suggested (Figure 6.5), remember to "don't just do something, stand there!" (i.e., wait for the storm to pass before attempting to introduce coping strategies). Once the child has been calm for a while, you can review together what happened and note what you saw him or her do that helped him or her feel calmer.

If you mess up: As noted before, no one is perfect all of the time. Sometimes, you may get sucked into a power struggle, escalate instead of de-escalate, lose your temper and say things you don't mean to say, or say you're going to impose a punishment

Table 6.3. Power struggles versus patience

The power struggle way	Another way
Teacher: Please start your math worksheet, Mary.	Teacher: Mary?
Child: In a minute	Child: Hold on, let me finish this page.
Teacher (annoyed): Mary I already asked you once. I need you to do it now.	Teacher (after brief wait, allowing Mary's attention to shift): Math will be starting in 5 minutes. What do you need to do?
Child: *No.*	Child (checking list): I need to get out my math book, worksheet, and pencil.
Teacher: Mary, if you don't start right now, you will get a zero and lose recess!	Teacher: You have 5 minutes—when do you want to start?
Child: Don't you have anything better to do than boss me around? (Throws worksheet and pencil.)	Child: I'll start now, but if I have time left over, can I go back to my book?
Teacher: Go to the principal!	Teacher: Sure, as long as you can put it away when it's time for math.

that isn't a part of your plan. When this happens, be forgiving and patient with yourself. This is a great opportunity for you to model for the child the important life skills of apologizing, admitting you made a mistake, and trying to make things right again. Avoid pretending it didn't happen; address it and move on.

PUTTING IT INTO ACTION
Coping Strategies Experiment

Make a game out of experimenting with the child to find coping strategies for both of you to use. Pick a time when you are both calm and try the strategies in Figure 6.10, plus any others that you both can think of.

PUTTING IT INTO ACTION
Feelings Thermometer

Help the child correctly identify the intensity of feelings (Figure 6.11). Start by practicing when the child is calm, and then you can move on to having him or her rate the intensity of his or her feelings when you suspect a coping strategy might be helpful. The strategies are much more likely to work if the child chooses when to use them rather than being told to use them!

Coping Strategies Experiment

Coping strategy	How much does this strategy help?					I like this strategy	I don't like this strategy
	1 None	2 A little	3 Some	4 A lot	5 I feel better		
Take five deep breaths.							
Close your eyes and think of a "happy place" (e.g., the beach).							
Close your eyes and think of your favorite activity.							
Run outside (maybe a lap around the house or ball field).							
Chew a piece of gum.							
Have a drink of water.							
Take a break.							
Read.							
Draw.							
Make your own strategy: _____							
Make your own strategy: _____							

Figure 6.10. Coping Strategies Experiment worksheet.

From Cannon, L., Kenworthy, L., Alexander, K.C., Werner, M.A., & Anthony, L.G. (2011). *Unstuck and on target!: An executive function curriculum to improve flexibility for children with autism spectrum disorders, research edition* (p. 73). Baltimore, MD: Paul H. Brookes Publishing Co.; adapted by permission. Copyright © 2011 by Paul H. Brookes Publishing Co., Inc. All rights reserved.

In *Solving Executive Function Challenges: Simple Ways to Get Kids with Autism Unstuck and on Target*, by Lauren Kenworthy, Laura Gutermuth Anthony, Katie C. Alexander, Monica Adler Werner, Lynn Cannon, & Lisa Greenman. (2014, Paul H. Brookes Publishing Co., Inc.)

Feelings Thermometer

How am I feeling right now?

1 Just Right	2 Warm	3 Too Warm	4 Hot	5 Red Hot

How do I wish to feel?

1 Just Right	2	3	4	5 Red Hot

Do I need to use a strategy?

Figure 6.11. Feelings Thermometer. (*Source:* Cannon, 2011.)

Problem 7: *Sometimes I can't tell what's willful misbehavior and what's ASD.*

Solution: *Think "can't, not won't."*

WHY THINK "CAN'T, NOT WON'T"?

Kunce and Mesibov[27] warned of the dangerous misunderstanding that can occur when people misinterpret the motivation for specific behaviors seen in children with ASD:

> A failure to understand how a child's typical behaviors reflect this disability can result in misperceptions such as viewing the child as noncompliant, willfully stubborn, or unmotivated, rather than confused, involved in repetitive routines, or focusing on less relevant aspects of the situation. (p. 227)

It is important to work extra hard to understand the perspectives of children with ASD, as they are so easily misunderstood. Sometimes, the gifts of autism, such as an expansive vocabulary or a remarkable memory, can increase the risk of misinterpretation: How can a kid who knows so much about physics not realize he's being rude when he points out that I am too fat? He actually believes that he is only stating a fact, and he is not trying to be hurtful at all. One can see this perspective when one tries to process the world through the filter of ASD, which relies on logical thinking more than emotional understanding. Ari Ne'eman points out that this perspective-taking exercise is one "that non-Autistic professionals [and parents] struggle with as much and perhaps far more than Autistic children struggle with understanding the perspectives of their non-Autistic peers" (personal communication). Empathy and understanding are essential; however, effective teaching and interventions to change behavior can only happen when the cause of the behavior is understood.

HOW TO THINK "CAN'T, NOT WON'T"

Is it "can't" or "won't"? Be a detective to figure out what causes a child's behaviors. In concrete terms, that means that when Johnny is standing at the dinner table saying that your beloved guest needs to get out of "his seat," rather than think of him as rude and embarrassing (both of which he may seem to be at that moment to the typical audience), ask yourself, "What does this say about what's difficult for him?" You wouldn't get mad at him for not being able to read without his glasses, so you shouldn't get mad at him for misreading social cues because of his ASD. If a child is not doing something, try to think of why he or she is not able to do the task. Table 6.4 explores commonly confused sources of behaviors in ASD.

Get help distinguishing the "can'ts" from the "won'ts." Although you possess a tremendous wealth of information about the child, professional evaluation can supplement that information. Evaluations can enhance your understanding and also inform decisions regarding additional services, both inside and outside of school. Evaluations should provide you with specific insights into how the child's brain processes and produces information that will

Table 6.4.   *Won't* versus *can't*

What looks like *won't*. . .	May actually be *can't*
"Oppositional, stubborn"	Cognitive inflexibility Protective effort to avoid overload
"Can do it when he *wants* to"	Difficulty shifting from one thing to another Trouble paying attention to what other people think is important
"Self-centered"	Impaired social problem solving/ Theory of Mind
"Doesn't care what others think"	Trouble understanding subtle social cues
"Doesn't try"	Difficulty getting started (initiation) Impaired planning and trouble generating new ideas
"Won't put good ideas on paper"	Poor fine motor skills, making writing hard Trouble organizing thoughts in a way that makes sense to a reader
"Sloppy, erratic"	Poor executive functioning, trouble monitoring Overload
"Won't control outbursts"	Overload Impaired inhibition or impulse control
"Prefers to be alone"	Impaired social understanding Needs a break from processing complex social information
"Doesn't care about what is important"	Natural ability to focus on details, harder time understanding the "big picture"

From Cannon, L., Kenworthy, L., Alexander, K.C., Werner, M.A., & Anthony, L.G. (2011). *Unstuck and on target!: An executive function curriculum to improve flexibility for children with autism spectrum disorders, research edition* (p. 8). Baltimore, MD: Paul H. Brookes Publishing Co.; adapted by permission.

help you to make sense of his or her behaviors. When the child is evaluated, become familiar with the findings and ask the evaluation professional(s) for help if you have trouble understanding the results. The results of an evaluation, in conjunction with your knowledge about the child, should yield the following:

- A specific, detailed account of his or her areas of difficulty and strengths (e.g., executive function [EF], social competencies, language, academic performance, motor skills)

- An explanation of how specific problem behaviors are related to differences in how he or she processes information and problem solves

- Specifics about how the child learns best (e.g., with visual or verbal information, through rote repetition, needs retrieval cues like multiple choice to recall information, hard to show what he or she knows by writing)

- Specifics about his or her perspective (e.g., dreams, likes and dislikes, fears, anxiety triggers, hopes, goals, beliefs, values)

- Concrete suggestions for how to leverage his or her strengths and interests to improve school, home, and social functions and to address problem behaviors

- Specific advice about what accommodations (i.e., changes in expectations or the environment) are appropriate for him or her

Advocate: Once you understand what is hard and easy for the child, sometimes you will need to educate others about his or her "can'ts" and help them respond appropriately. Often, parents or others are reluctant to tell people that a child has a disability. Usually, a child with ASD will appear different in some way to the adults and children with whom he interacts, and if you don't give these differences a name, others will. Unfortunately, some of those names (e.g., mean, rude, has bad parents) are much worse and more stigmatizing than ASD. You may choose not to use ASD as the frame, but instead use some other explanation that helps people understand and respond to the child better. Sometimes it helps to frame the issue as an expression of a child's gifts. For example, "Sam is such an expert on bugs, he sometimes forgets that other people don't love them as much as he does. Give him a signal if he talks about them too long for you."

- Parents must actively advocate for their children to receive an individualized education program (IEP) at school that includes appropriate accommodations as well as goals for the child's education. See Appendix B for sample IEP language. It is daunting for most parents to confront the often 10 or more school personnel who attend IEP meetings about ways the school needs to better understand and serve their child. Parents should consider taking an advocate or a relative with them and remember that they are the expert on the child.

- Share the vocabulary that works well for the child between home and school. Teachers and parents are usually excited to use effective terminology. Teachers and school therapists will have important information to share with parents and private therapists, and vice versa. Use IEP and other school meetings to get everyone on the same page in terms of understanding how the child learns, what the major stumbling blocks are for the child, and what works to avoid them. Make sure that all members of the child's team, including parents, share their understanding of what are can'ts and what are won'ts for the child.

- Share information about ASD with other relatives, school staff, and community members if you think it will help them to be more supportive of the child. You may also have to be explicit about gifts and/or triggers (e.g., "Mary is really smart, but she has a hard time reading emotions. You will have to tell her explicitly how you feel and why." Or "Sam will react badly if he thinks you are talking down to him. He has a terrific vocabulary and will understand anything you say to him directly."). See Putting It into Action: Sample Letter of Explanation later in this section.

Identify others who can also advocate, support, and coach. A "safe address" is a person who understands the child and ASD and is available to the child on an as-needed basis to review difficult interactions with others, explain confusing situations, and advocate for the child's needs. The safe address also seeks out the child on a regular basis to monitor, teach, and actively coach skills. A parent may be the safe address at home, but the child will need another safe address at school. This person can be any approved adult with whom the child identifies and feels comfortable, and who understands what are can'ts versus won'ts for the child. It will not be possible for a child with ASD to learn to be more flexible without such support. The confusion, social isolation, teasing, and bullying experienced by children with ASD without social support are traumatic events that increase anxiety, decrease flexibility, and impair learning of all kinds.

Encourage self-advocacy. A crucial predictor of success in adulthood is knowing how and when to ask for help. You may start by giving a child scripts for self-advocacy. Some examples of scripts may be "I need help with *X*." "It is hard for me to listen to you when it is noisy; can we talk somewhere else?" "I don't understand what you mean." "Sometimes I need to take a break, but I still want to play with you."

Be careful not to create limitations or "can't" situations by over-supporting the child.

- *Use the Socratic method,* a method of teaching that involves using questions to stimulate independent and critical thinking. In an effort to reduce overload and help children move through a task, it is easy to get caught up in the "do it for them" mode. For example, we see that the task will require a pair of scissors, so we quickly hand the child a pair of scissors. Although we are being helpful in the moment, we are often preventing our children from becoming independent problem solvers. As you begin to employ the Socratic method to increase a child's independence, think of skills and tasks that he or she already knows how to do. For example, it is time for dinner and you have been working on setting the table. Pose the question, "We are having soup. What do we need to eat with?" By asking questions, you engage the child's critical thinking skills and get him or her in the habit of independently solving problems.

- *Know when to back off.* In addition to thinking about how to incorporate the Socratic method, it is also important to think about the types of prompts you are providing. As discussed earlier in Chapter 2, it is essential to withdraw your coaching in order for the child to develop and demonstrate independence with a skill. Otherwise, you could be creating more can'ts by doing too much for the child and making him or her more dependent on you. You may have to pause for a long time while waiting for a child with ASD to come up with a response or a solution, but it is worth the waiting in the long run if you can resist jumping in.

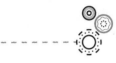 **PUTTING IT INTO ACTION**
*An Overview of ASD
for Friends and Family*

Give friends and family members an explanation of ASD and how it may affect behavior: ASDs are a specific group of social, communication, and restricted or repetitive behaviors that affect an individual's development and interactions with others. Possible causes of ASD include genetics, prenatal infection or exposures, and developmental differences in the brain. Extensive research has shown that ASDs are brain-based disorders that are *not* caused by bad parenting. Children with ASDs may act atypically, not because they want to be difficult, but rather because they are just being themselves and even responding adaptively to the environment. The following are common symptoms and strengths of ASDs, though no one child will have all of these symptoms or strengths:

Social Interactions
- Wants to make friends but doesn't know how
- Often doesn't "get" social cues or understand unwritten social rules
- Doesn't usually make eye contact
- Doesn't always understand facial expressions and body language
- Makes inappropriate facial expressions

Social Interactions
- Has the same emotions as everyone else, but expresses them differently
- Behaves with honesty and integrity
- Is genuine and open
- Is very willing to follow clear rules and schedules
- Has a charming innocence
- Often has a great sense of humor

Communication
- May have difficulty with spoken language, especially pronouns ("I," "you"), figures of speech, and sarcasm
- Uses memorized phrases and quotes
- May not respond when spoken to
- Speaks in an unusual tone of voice (e.g., sounding bored)

Thinking
- Memorizes information, especially visual information, easily
- Has an unusually strong long-term memory
- Pays strong attention to details, especially visual details
- Has an excellent sense of direction
- Works precisely and is a perfectionist
- Thinks and solves problems logically
- Able to maintain focus on interesting activities well
- May have passionate interests
- May have special talents

Behavior
- Has over- or undersensitive senses of smell, taste, sight, sound, pain, or touch
- Shows repetitive body movements
- Shows limited imaginative play
- Strongly opposes change; likes routines
- Has intense tantrums
- Has narrow, intense interests
- Can't move off of a single topic of interest
- Is easily overwhelmed, even in small groups
- Notices details but can miss the "big picture"

Ways to Help
- Be sensitive to the fact that children with ASDs have the same feelings as everyone else. They are hurt just as much as "typical" children by being excluded. Ask how you can include him or her in activities you are planning.
- Don't be offended if the child doesn't make eye contact, sounds annoyed or bored, or ignores you. These behaviors are caused by physical differences in his or her brain, not by a bad attitude.
- Understand that bright lights, loud sounds, and strong smells can be so overwhelming they are painful to the child. Many

tantrums are caused by these sensory differences.

- Use clear, literal language (i.e., mean what you say and say what you mean) and stick to predictable schedules around the child.

- Recognize that, although people with ASDs have a different way of being in the world, they still have tremendous potential.

PUTTING IT INTO ACTION
Sample Letter of Explanation

To create a letter of explanation, you should be as specific as you can, particularly addressing the following:

- Predicting possible behavior (e.g., "He doesn't like to be touched.")
- Providing an explanation for that behavior (e.g., "Because of his ASD, some touch feels painful.")
- Letting the parents or children know what to do in the situation to be helpful (e.g., "Don't stand or jostle too closely," or "If he does get upset, just back up a bit and wait for him to calm down.")

You may want to send letters to participants (e.g., classmates, church members, neighbors, co-workers before the company picnic) when you would like the child to be included in a community event. Figure 6.12 shows an example of a letter.

Problem 8: *The child would rather spend time in front of a screen than be with people.*

Solution: *Technology can be your ally.*

WHY MAKE TECHNOLOGY MY ALLY?

Technology often gets a bad reputation, because some children over-focus on computers and other "screen time" activities. However, harnessing that interest can make a child with ASD more available for the hard work that learning flexibility and EF skills requires. When properly controlled (see the list item Taming the Beast later in this section), computers of all types can provide

Dear Soccer Team Parents,

Our son Gabriel is a new child on the soccer team, and his father and I wanted to tell you some things about him. This team will be Gabriel's first experience with a sports team in an inclusive environment. Gabriel has an autism spectrum disorder that causes him to have a great deal of difficulty modulating his behavior. He feels things very intensely, and it is often hard for him to control his reactions, to accept things that he disagrees with, or to see things from someone else's perspective. Gabriel also has difficulty with social interactions and will sometimes say things that are embarrassing or disrespectful without realizing it. Gabriel's sophisticated language skills often mask his disability, and so his impulsive words or actions may appear willful or rude. We want you to know that these things are, for the most part, symptoms of problems that we are working together with him to manage and overcome.

We're quite open to talking about all this, so please feel free. And we want to tell you that Gabriel has lots of wonderful qualities as well: he has a great sense of humor, he can be extraordinarily kind and compassionate, he's an amazing reader, and he's a very enthusiastic soccer player. Gabriel is a big presence, in ways that are wonderful and in ways that are challenging, and we hope this will be a good experience all around. If he does have tough times on the field, you may want to let your children know that Gabriel has a disability because his brain works differently. Sometimes he says and does things he doesn't really mean, but it doesn't mean that he's a bad kid. Gabriel certainly recognizes this himself, and in our experience, the disability framework is helpful to children. Thanks so much for spending the time to take this all in. And here's hoping for sunshine on Saturday!

—Gabe's mom and dad

Figure 6.12.   Sample letter of explanation.

natural supports to a child's executive system. Mass marketing increases the appeal of gadgets; children like smartphones, tablet computers, and laptops, among other electronic devices. More important, computers, large and small, are appealing to many children with ASD specifically because they support exactly those abilities that are typically weakest in ASD. By supporting the following skills, computers allow children to tackle one problem at a time and avoid being overloaded with social, executive, and motor demands simultaneously.

- *Motor skills:* Computers, especially touch screens, lower fine-motor demands on children who often resist traditional "pen and paper" tasks.

- *Organization:* Computers provide an automatic, neutral system for making checklists, setting reminders, and organizing information and tasks. This means the already overloaded child does not have to tolerate "nagging" adults to remind him or her of things. Furthermore, the child can be part of creating his or her own organizational systems on a computer, which increases his or her sense of ownership and motivation. Technology can also help avoid overload by storing information in easily accessible formats, such as one-touch pop-up checklists, reminders on calendars, and self-monitoring prompts.

- *Flexibility:* Computers can be formatted to the specifications of the user and, once set up, will consistently look the same way. Unlike getting directions from a parent or a teacher, the same steps are used each time you carry out an activity on a computer.

- *Social skills:* Technology does not add any social demands to complicate task completion.

- *Processing speed:* Unlike when interacting with a person, the child gets to set the pace of the interaction when working with a computer. The child can move quickly through familiar material but is not rushed when he or she encounters more difficult material. Social communication via technology (e.g., social networks, texting) slows down interactions and allows time to think and reflect. Using online communication methods can foster early social interactions by encouraging reciprocity, appropriateness, and relationship building without the pressure of real-time interactions.

- *Motivation:* Children with ASD can be most effectively motivated by nonsocial rewards related to their special interests or, often, technology. Technology can be the reward, with programs that support developing skills with attractive games. This is quite common in many learning programs and should be harnessed for children using technology to support their EF skills.

HOW TO MAKE TECHNOLOGY YOUR ALLY

The number of applications for technology is growing every day, as are the variety of flexible and portable computers. "Apps" for handheld devices are also exploding in popularity and availability. A book such as this cannot be up to date on details, but can offer a few basic principles regarding the uses of technology.

Handheld devices provide organizing routines, schedules, and lists.

- Although all of these functions can be done on a laptop, a handheld device is less cumbersome.

- Calendars on handheld devices are more than electronic visual schedules. They can be set with reminders that are tied to checklists (e.g., a reminder set for the end of class that prompts the use of the "end of class checklist").

- Children can use that same calendar to put in new "appointments" about homework or meetings with teachers and therapists.

- Handhelds also help with a big problem for many children who can learn to write down an assignment on the day it is assigned, but not to write it again in their calendars on the days they have to work on it or the day it is due. A handheld can be programmed to automatically prompt the child to complete these steps.

- Children who struggle with disorganization often have the greatest difficulty applying what they know in real time. For example, they can demonstrate full mastery of a routine for recording homework at the end of class, but will often forget to do so. Handheld devices, like computers, have calendars with alarms that can be set to go off at key times, reminding a child to implement a routine, keep an appointment, or check in with a teacher.

Laptops and tablets support notetaking and writing. A computer can take pressure off the child and reduce overload or even refusal of writing tasks, allowing him or her to tackle the all-important skill of learning to express his or her ideas clearly.

- The laptop and the handheld device are the new prosthetics for children who hate handwriting and, even after years of occupational therapy, continue to write illegibly or with great effort. Many of those same children who struggle with a pen and paper are agile with a keyboard (some hunt and peck at remarkable speeds) or with two-finger texting. Reducing the handwriting load can lead to greater output in written tasks, an already challenging area for children struggling to be organized and flexible.

- Templates for taking notes, such as grids that help organize main idea and supporting information (the two-column note system), can help a child attend to the material as well as organize the information, even as the teacher is talking.

- Computers also have built-in programs to cue children to make needed spelling and grammar corrections and allow a child to revise and still produce a good-looking document, in contrast to the messy, torn, and much-erased final copies often produced when writing by hand.

Computers are effective at teaching new skills. Computer programs for teaching typing skills, math, how to recognize faces and expressions, vocabulary, and many other skills are often particularly motivating to children with ASD. One reason for this is that they provide richer visual information than is available in traditional teaching. For this reason, they are also excellent tools for researching topics and expanding knowledge bases. Another big advantage of computer-based curricula is that they are self-paced, allowing a child to work quickly when he or she can and slow down learning when necessary.

Computers help children present information effectively. Power-Point and other software enable a child to present visual as well as verbal information effectively. Whether producing words or pictures, computers enable the child to produce and edit his or her work without evidence of shaky fine motor control or messy erasing, resulting in a product of which you both will feel genuinely proud.

Handhelds are increasingly able to support children with self-monitoring. Handhelds provide easily accessible formats for a child to rate his or her feelings or the difficulty of a task, or to engage in other self-monitoring. Software is available that provides user-friendly, individualized checklists that allow children to monitor their moods, their reactions to different situations, and their use of their coping strategies. That information can then be downloaded, graphed, and discussed with a child as "neutral" data that the child has generated, as opposed to "judgmental comments" from an adult. A system that simultaneously has an adult observing the child and doing the same ratings can provide feedback to the child by giving him or her comparative data about how he or she behaved while working on a difficult task.

- -

Taming the Beast: education and parental controls: There are downsides to the use of technology that must be carefully addressed.

- *Many children have trouble ending a computer session,* especially if they are playing games, and sometimes they use computers to view inappropriate and/or distracting Internet sites, programs, or activities. It is important to control the time a child spends on the computer and what he or she has access to. Here again, technology is on your side, as a plethora of computer control programs have been developed in recent years that enable you to control what programs and Internet sites a child can navigate to, during what times of day, and for how long. Many parents find software that automatically turns off a computer after a set period of time to be especially helpful, and it is important to use sophisticated Internet controls to prevent access to specific sites, games, or the Internet in general.

- *Computers can offer access to content on the Internet that can be harmful or even illegal.* The Internet controls described earlier in this section will help you monitor and limit what a child has access to. In addition, explicitly educate the child about the dangers of social networking on computers. Explain that what he or she posts on sites such as Facebook is permanent, public information and that participating or even being an innocent computer bystander in sexual, bullying, or other comments on the Internet implicates him or her in the activity. Warn the child that the Internet gives predators easy access to him or her. In keeping with the simultaneously positive and negative power of the Internet, there are several good Internet education and awareness programs available on the Internet.

- *Some schools prohibit the use of handheld devices,* but this problem can usually be addressed through the 504 or IEP process and explicit recognition that such devices are used as important assistive technology for the child.

- *Technology is expensive and comes in increasingly small sizes,* which means that it can be easily lost. This is an unavoidable problem, but for many children with ASD the benefits of technology outweigh the costs. When these devices are used for therapeutic reasons, it can be possible to find funding for them through grants, insurance, or nonprofit organizations. You may want to buy insurance for the device and/or sign up for a program that can help you locate the device in the event of loss or theft.

 PUTTING IT INTO ACTION

Research Apps and Computer Programs

There are many useful apps and computer supports, and they change frequently. Do some research online, at your local computer or electronics store, or by asking other parents of children with ASD. Investigate what programs are available to help children track homework, complete daily living routines, keep appointments, organize writing, enlarge print, transfer voice to print, transfer print to voice, monitor and record how they are feeling, gain access to coping and EF strategies and scripts, and so forth.

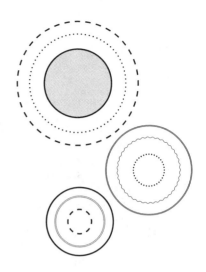

Endnotes

1. Robison, J.E. (2011). *Be different: Adventures of a free-range Aspergian*. New York, NY: Crown Archetype.

2. Hill, E.L. (2004). Evaluating the theory of executive dysfunction in autism. *Developmental Review, 24*(2), 189–233. doi:10.1016/j.dr.2004.01.001

3. Kenworthy, L., Yerys, B.E., Anthony, L., & Wallace, G.L. (2008). Understanding executive control in autism spectrum disorders in the lab and in the real world. *Neuropsychology Review, 18*(4), 320–338. doi:10.1007/s11065–008–9077–7

4. Pennington, B.F., & Ozonoff, S. (1996). Executive functions and developmental psychopathology. *Journal of Child Psychology and Psychiatry, 37*(1), 51–87. doi:10.1111/j.1469–7610.1996.tb01380.x

5. Sergeant, J.A., Geurts, H., & Oosterlaan, J. (2002). How specific is a deficit of executive functioning for attention-deficit/hyperactivity disorder? *Behavioural Brain Research, 130*(1–2), 3–28. doi:10.1016/S0166–4328(01)00430–2

6. Solomon, M. *et al.* (2009). The neural substrates of cognitive control deficits in autism spectrum disorders. *Neuropsychologia, 47,* 2515–2526.

7. Huttenlocher, P.R. (1990). Morphometric study of human cerebral cortex development. *Neuropsychologia 28,* 517–527.

8. OSEP Center on Positive Behavioral Interventions and Supports Technical Assistance (2013). Effective schoolwide interventions. Retrieved December 5, 2013, from http://www.pbis.org/

9. Feeney, T.J. (2010). Structured flexibility: The use of context-sensitive self-regulatory scripts to support young persons with acquired brain injury and behavioral difficulties. *Journal of Head Trauma Rehabilitation, 25,* 416–425.

10. Ylvisaker, M. (2006). *Tutorial: Self-regulation/executive function routines after TBI.* Retrieved from http://www.projectlearnet.org/tutorials/sr_ef_routines.html

11. Kenworthy, L., Anthony, L.G., Naiman, D.Q., Cannon, L., Wills, M.C., Werner, M.A., . . . Wallace, G.L. (in press). Executive function versus social .skills interventions for children on the autism spectrum: An effectiveness trial. *Journal of Child Psychology and Psychiatry.*

12. Polatajko, H., & Mandich, A. (2004). *Enabling occupation in children: The cognitive orientation to daily occupational performance (CO-OP) approach.* Ottawa, Canada: CAOT Publications.

13. Patterson, G.R. (2002). The early development of coercive family process. In J.B. Reid, G.R. Patterson, & J. Snyder (Eds.), *Antisocial behavior in children and adolescents: A developmental analysis and model for intervention* (pp. 25–44). Washington, DC: American Psychological Association. doi:10.1037/10468-002

14. Shores, R.E., Gunter, P.L., & Jack, S.L. (1993). Classroom management strategies: Are they setting events for coercion? *Behavioral Disorders, 18*(2), 92–102.

15. Flora, S.R. (2000). Praise's magic reinforcement ratio: Five to one gets the job done. *The Behavior Analyst Today, 1*(4), 64–69.

16. Frith, U., & Happé, F. (1994). Autism: Beyond "theory of mind." *Cognition, 50*(1–3), 115–132. doi:10.1016/0010-0277(94)90024-8

17. Kenworthy, L., Black, D., Wallace, G., Ahluvalia, T., Wagner, A., & Sirian, L. (2005). Disorganization: The forgotten executive dysfunction in high functioning autism spectrum disorders. *Developmental Neuropsychology, 28*, 809–827.

18. Baldo, J.V., Dronkers, N.F., Wilkins, D., Ludy, C., Raskin, P., & Kim, J. (2005). Is problem solving dependent on language? *Brain and Language, 92*(3), 240–250. doi:10.1016/j.bandl.2004.06.103

19. Vygotsky, L.S. (1962). *Thought and language.* Oxford, England: Wiley. doi:10.1037/11193-000

20. Wallace, G.L., Silvers, J.A., Martin, A., & Kenworthy, L.E. (2009). Brief report: Further evidence for inner speech deficits in autism spectrum disorders. *Journal of Autism and Developmental Disorders, 39*(12), 1735–1739. doi:10.1007/s10803-009-0802-8

21. Russell, J., Jarrold, C., & Hood, B. (1999). Two intact executive capacities in children with autism: Implications for the core executive dysfunctions in the disorder. *Journal of Autism and Developmental Disorders, 29*(2), 103–112. doi:10.1023/A:1023084425406

22. Whitehouse, A.O., Maybery, M.T., & Durkin, K. (2006). Inner speech impairments in autism. *Journal of Child Psychology and Psychiatry, 47*(8), 857–865. doi:10.1111/j.1469-7610.2006.01624.x

23. Joseph, R.M., Steele, S.D., Meyer, E., & Tager-Flusberg, H. (2005). Self-ordered pointing in children with autism: Failure to use verbal mediation in the service of working memory? *Neuropsychologia, 43*, 1400–1411.

24. Abbeduto, L., Seltzer, M.M., Shattuck, P., Krauss, M., Orsmond, G., & Murphy, M. (2004). Psychological well-being and coping in mothers of youths with autism, Down syndrome, or fragile X syndrome. *American Journal of Mental Retardation, 109*, 237–254.

25. Lounds, J.J., Seltzer, M.M., Greenberg, J.S., & Shattuck, P. (2007). Transition and change in adolescents and young adults with autism: Longitudinal effects on maternal well-being. *American Journal on Mental Retardation, 112*, 401–417.

26. Boyd, B. (2003). *Parenting a child with Asperger syndrome: 200 tips and strategies.* London, England: Jessica Kingsley Publishers.

27. Kunce, L., & Mesibov, G.B. (1998). Educational approaches to high-functioning autism and Asperger syndrome. In E. Schopler, G.B. Mesibov, & L.J. Kunce (Eds.), *Asperger syndrome or high-functioning autism?* (pp. 227–261). New York, NY: Plenum Press.

Appendix

Sample Goal, Plan, Do, Checks

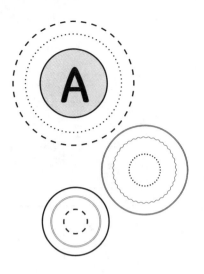

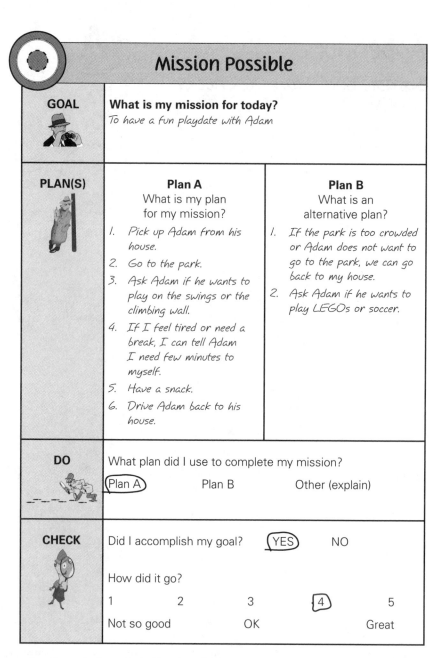

Mission Possible

GOAL	**What is my mission for today?** *To have a fun playdate with Adam*

PLAN(S)	**Plan A** What is my plan for my mission?

Plan A — What is my plan for my mission?

1. *Pick up Adam from his house.*
2. *Go to the park.*
3. *Ask Adam if he wants to play on the swings or the climbing wall.*
4. *If I feel tired or need a break, I can tell Adam I need few minutes to myself.*
5. *Have a snack.*
6. *Drive Adam back to his house.*

Plan B — What is an alternative plan?

1. *If the park is too crowded or Adam does not want to go to the park, we can go back to my house.*
2. *Ask Adam if he wants to play LEGOs or soccer.*

DO — What plan did I use to complete my mission?

(Plan A)   Plan B   Other (explain)

CHECK — Did I accomplish my goal?   (YES)   NO

How did it go?

1	2	3	4	5
Not so good		OK		Great

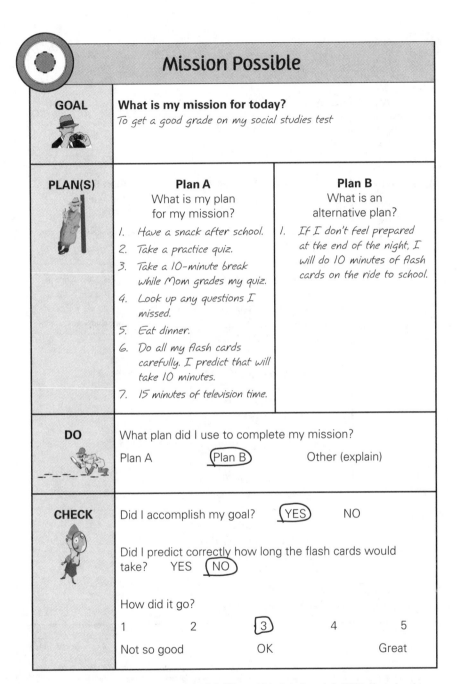

Mission Possible

GOAL

What is my mission for today?

To get a good grade on my social studies test

PLAN(S)

Plan A What is my plan for my mission?	**Plan B** What is an alternative plan?
1. *Have a snack after school.* 2. *Take a practice quiz.* 3. *Take a 10-minute break while Mom grades my quiz.* 4. *Look up any questions I missed.* 5. *Eat dinner.* 6. *Do all my flash cards carefully. I predict that will take 10 minutes.* 7. *15 minutes of television time.*	1. *If I don't feel prepared at the end of the night, I will do 10 minutes of flash cards on the ride to school.*

DO

What plan did I use to complete my mission?

Plan A (Plan B) Other (explain)

CHECK

Did I accomplish my goal? (YES) NO

Did I predict correctly how long the flash cards would take? YES (NO)

How did it go?

1	2	3	4	5
Not so good		OK		Great

From Cannon, L., Kenworthy, L., Alexander, K.C., Werner, M.A., & Anthony, L.G. (2011). *Unstuck and on target!: An executive function curriculum to improve flexibility for children with autism spectrum disorders, research edition* (pp. 140, 143). Baltimore, MD: Paul H. Brookes Publishing Co.; adapted by permission. Copyright © 2011 by Paul H. Brookes Publishing Co., Inc. All rights reserved.

In *Solving Executive Function Challenges: Simple Ways to Get Kids with Autism Unstuck and on Target*, by Lauren Kenworthy, Laura Gutermuth Anthony, Katie C. Alexander, Monica Adler Werner, Lynn Cannon, & Lisa Greenman. (2014, Paul H. Brookes Publishing Co., Inc.)

Mission Possible

GOAL	**What is my mission for today?** *To finish my homework calmly while staying focused*

	Plan A	Plan B
PLAN(S)	**Plan A** What is my plan for my mission?	**Plan B** What is an alternative plan?

<table>
<tr><td></td>
<td>

1. *Have a snack after school.*
2. *Spend 15 minutes doing something that helps me feel more relaxed, but not television.*
3. *Review my homework assignments and decide in what order I want to do them.*
4. *Decide when I might want to take breaks. I predict that my work and breaks will take 30 minutes.*
5. *Keep my feelings thermometer with me (Figure 6.11).*
6. *Stay focused on one assignment at a time and take my breaks.*
7. *As I complete assignments, put them back in my folder to go back to school.*
8. *Once I've finished, put my folder in my backpack.*
9. *Watch 15 minutes television.*

</td>
<td>

1. *If an assignment feels too tricky, I can ask my mom or dad for help.*

    If I feel stuck on an assignment, I can take a break from it, do another assignment, and come back to it later.

</td>
</tr>
</table>

(continued)

From Cannon, L., Kenworthy, L., Alexander, K.C., Werner, M.A., & Anthony, L.G. (2011). *Unstuck and on target!: An executive function curriculum to improve flexibility for children with autism spectrum disorders, research edition* (pp. 140, 143). Baltimore, MD: Paul H. Brookes Publishing Co.; adapted by permission. Copyright © 2011 by Paul H. Brookes Publishing Co., Inc. All rights reserved.

In *Solving Executive Function Challenges: Simple Ways to Get Kids with Autism Unstuck and on Target*, by Lauren Kenworthy, Laura Gutermuth Anthony, Katie C. Alexander, Monica Adler Werner, Lynn Cannon, & Lisa Greenman. (2014, Paul H. Brookes Publishing Co., Inc.)

(continued)

DO	What plan did I use to complete my mission?
	(Plan A) Plan B Other (explain)
CHECK	Did I accomplish my goal? (YES) NO
	Did I predict correctly how long my homework and breaks would take? (YES) NO
	How did it go?
	1 2 3 4 (5)
	Not so good OK Great

Mission Possible

GOAL	**What is my mission for today?**
	To get ready in the morning and on my way to school on time

PLAN(S)

Plan A What is my plan for my mission?	**Plan B** What is an alternative plan?

1. The night before, I will
   a. Choose my outfit (including my underwear, socks, and shoes) and set it on my desk.
   b. Plan breakfast with my dad and write down the menu.
   c. Check my backpack to make sure everything is in it, and set it by the door.
   d. Put my comics by my chair in case I have time to read.
2. I think I can finish my morning routine in 45 minutes (e.g., eat breakfast, brush my teeth, wash my face and hands, and get dressed).
3. I will use my morning routine checklist.
4. I will plan for an extra 15 minutes just in case something doesn't go the way I hoped.
5. If I've finished my morning routine by 7:50, I can read comics until the bus arrives.
6. Grab my backpack when I leave the house.
	1. If I get stuck, my mom can help me use my routine checklist.
	2. My mom will let me know how much time I have left before the bus arrives.

(continued)

From Cannon, L., Kenworthy, L., Alexander, K.C., Werner, M.A., & Anthony, L.G. (2011). *Unstuck and on target!: An executive function curriculum to improve flexibility for children with autism spectrum disorders, research edition* (pp. 140, 143). Baltimore, MD: Paul H. Brookes Publishing Co.; adapted by permission. Copyright © 2011 by Paul H. Brookes Publishing Co., Inc. All rights reserved.

In *Solving Executive Function Challenges: Simple Ways to Get Kids with Autism Unstuck and on Target*, by Lauren Kenworthy, Laura Gutermuth Anthony, Katie C. Alexander, Monica Adler Werner, Lynn Cannon, & Lisa Greenman. (2014, Paul H. Brookes Publishing Co., Inc.)

DO	What plan did I use to complete my mission? Plan A Plan B (Other)(explain) *Need a Plan C*
CHECK	Did I accomplish my goal? YES (NO) Did I predict correctly how long my morning routine would take? YES (NO) How did it go? (1) 2 3 4 5 Not so good OK Great

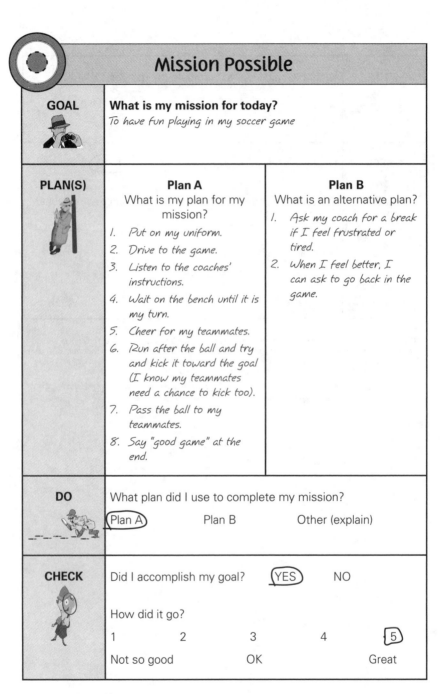

Mission Possible

GOAL

What is my mission for today?

To have fun playing in my soccer game

PLAN(S)

Plan A
What is my plan for my mission?

1. Put on my uniform.
2. Drive to the game.
3. Listen to the coaches' instructions.
4. Wait on the bench until it is my turn.
5. Cheer for my teammates.
6. Run after the ball and try and kick it toward the goal (I know my teammates need a chance to kick too).
7. Pass the ball to my teammates.
8. Say "good game" at the end.

Plan B
What is an alternative plan?

1. Ask my coach for a break if I feel frustrated or tired.
2. When I feel better, I can ask to go back in the game.

DO

What plan did I use to complete my mission?

(Plan A)   Plan B   Other (explain)

CHECK

Did I accomplish my goal?   (YES)   NO

How did it go?

1   2   3   4   (5)

Not so good   OK   Great

Mission Possible

GOAL	**What is my mission for today?** *To have fun at recess*
PLAN(S)	**Plan A** What is my plan for my mission? *1. Ask Sarah if she wants to go on the climbing wall.* **Plan B** What is an alternative plan? *1. Ask Ben if he wants to go on the slide.* **Plan C** What is an alternative plan? *1. Ask Oliver if he wants to play basketball.* **Plan D** What is an alternative plan? *1. Swing by myself.*
DO	What plan did I use to complete my mission? Plan A Plan B (Other) (explain) *Plan D*
CHECK	Did I accomplish my goal? YES (NO) How did it go? (1) 2 3 4 5 Not so good OK Great

Mission Possible

GOAL 	**What is my mission for today?** *To finish my biography assignment on time and follow the directions so that I can get a good grade*

PLAN(S) 	**Plan A** What is my plan?	**Plan B** What is an alternative plan?

Plan A — What is my plan?

1. Pay attention to the teacher when she gives the directions for the biography.
2. Copy the directions in my notebook.
3. Write down the due date.
4. The rough draft is due in 1 week, and the final draft is due in 2 weeks. Remember that the reason I do a rough draft is so that my teacher can help me improve my writing for the final draft.
5. The topic is My Hero.
6. Read two sources (not Wikipedia).
7. List my sources and use information from each of them in the biography.

Plan B — What is an alternative plan?

1. If I run out of time in class, I can work on this assignment at home.
2. If I get stuck, I can ask my teacher for help.

DO 	**What plan did I use to complete my mission?** (Plan A) Plan B Other (explain) *Except Step 6*

(continued)

(continued)

CHECK	Did I accomplish my goal? (YES) NO
	How did it go?
	1 2 3 {4} 5
	Not so good OK Great

Mission Possible

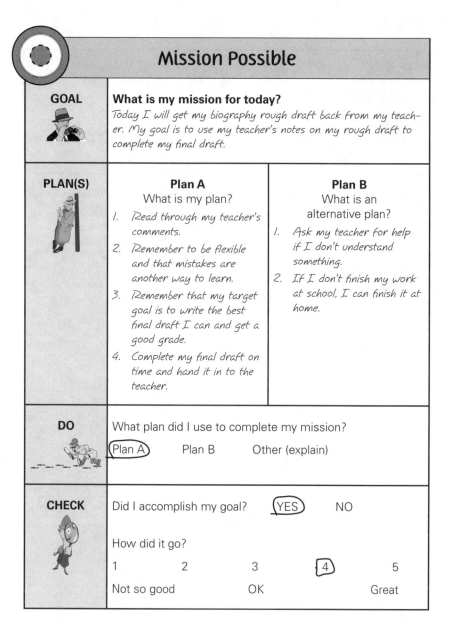

GOAL

What is my mission for today?

Today I will get my biography rough draft back from my teacher. My goal is to use my teacher's notes on my rough draft to complete my final draft.

PLAN(S)

Plan A
What is my plan?

1. *Read through my teacher's comments.*
2. *Remember to be flexible and that mistakes are another way to learn.*
3. *Remember that my target goal is to write the best final draft I can and get a good grade.*
4. *Complete my final draft on time and hand it in to the teacher.*

Plan B
What is an alternative plan?

1. *Ask my teacher for help if I don't understand something.*
2. *If I don't finish my work at school, I can finish it at home.*

DO

What plan did I use to complete my mission?

(Plan A)   Plan B   Other (explain)

CHECK

Did I accomplish my goal?   (YES)   NO

How did it go?

1	2	3	4	5
Not so good		OK		Great

From Cannon, L., Kenworthy, L., Alexander, K.C., Werner, M.A., & Anthony, L.G. (2011). *Unstuck and on target!: An executive function curriculum to improve flexibility for children with autism spectrum disorders, research edition* (pp. 140, 143). Baltimore, MD: Paul H. Brookes Publishing Co.; adapted by permission.
Copyright © 2011 by Paul H. Brookes Publishing Co., Inc. All rights reserved.

In *Solving Executive Function Challenges: Simple Ways to Get Kids with Autism Unstuck and on Target*, by Lauren Kenworthy, Laura Gutermuth Anthony, Katie C. Alexander, Monica Adler Werner, Lynn Cannon, & Lisa Greenman. (2014, Paul H. Brookes Publishing Co., Inc.)

Mission Possible

GOAL	**What is my mission for today?** To create a notebook for all of my schoolwork

PLAN(S)	**Plan A** What is my plan?	**Plan B** What is an alternative plan?
	1. Pick out a notebook that I like from the choices my mom or dad gives me. 2. Pick out a different-colored folder for each class. 3. The color of folder that I pick will be the color for any special supplies needed (like a spiral notebook) for the class (when there are choices). This is called color coding. 4. Put all supplies in the notebook that can go in the notebook, keeping items for each class together. 5. Label each section and the supplies in that section. 6. Celebrate getting organized and ready for school with a special activity.	1. If I can't find the color I want, I can add that color to my notebook in a different way (like with the color of my pencils or using that color to label). 2. If I need help, I can ask my parent.

DO	What plan did I use to complete my mission? Plan A (Plan B) Other (explain)

(continued)

From Cannon, L., Kenworthy, L., Alexander, K.C., Werner, M.A., & Anthony, L.G. (2011). *Unstuck and on target!: An executive function curriculum to improve flexibility for children with autism spectrum disorders, research edition* (pp. 140, 143). Baltimore, MD: Paul H. Brookes Publishing Co.; adapted by permission. Copyright © 2011 by Paul H. Brookes Publishing Co., Inc. All rights reserved.

In *Solving Executive Function Challenges: Simple Ways to Get Kids with Autism Unstuck and on Target*, by Lauren Kenworthy, Laura Gutermuth Anthony, Katie C. Alexander, Monica Adler Werner, Lynn Cannon, & Lisa Greenman. (2014, Paul H. Brookes Publishing Co., Inc.)

(continued)

CHECK	Did I accomplish my goal? (YES) NO
	How did it go?
	1 2 [3] 4 5
	Not so good OK Great

Mission Possible

GOAL	**What is my mission for today?**
	To be a good student who follows the directions for my assignments with only some help and gets my work done on time

PLAN(S)	**Plan A** What is my plan?	**Plan B** What is an alternative plan?
	1. Always copy the directions for an assignment. 2. Always write the due date where my due dates go in my notebook. 3. Break my assignment into the steps my teacher gives me and decide when I need to do each section so that it's done on time. 4. Start as soon as it is time to start so that I can get my work done on time. 5. Be ready to be flexible and compromise so that I can get some of what I want and get a good grade by following the assignment directions. 6. Check the clock to see how much time I have. 7. Stay on target when working and avoid distractions that could interest me. 8. Keep checking to see what the time is. 9. Be flexible and use my teacher's guidance to improve my work.	1. I can use a timer to help me stay on task if I'm having trouble. I can set the timer for 10 minutes, and every time it goes off, ask myself if I am on target. If I'm not on target, I can look back at my plan to get on target. 2. I can ask my teacher for help if something is tricky.

(continued)

In *Solving Executive Function Challenges: Simple Ways to Get Kids with Autism Unstuck and on Target*, by Lauren Kenworthy, Laura Gutermuth Anthony, Katie C. Alexander, Monica Adler Werner, Lynn Cannon, & Lisa Greenman. (2014, Paul H. Brookes Publishing Co., Inc.)

(continued)

DO	What plan did I use to complete my mission? Plan A Plan B (Other)(explain) *Need a Plan C*
CHECK	Did I accomplish my goal? YES (NO) How did it go? (1) 2 3 4 5 Not so good OK Great

Mission Possible

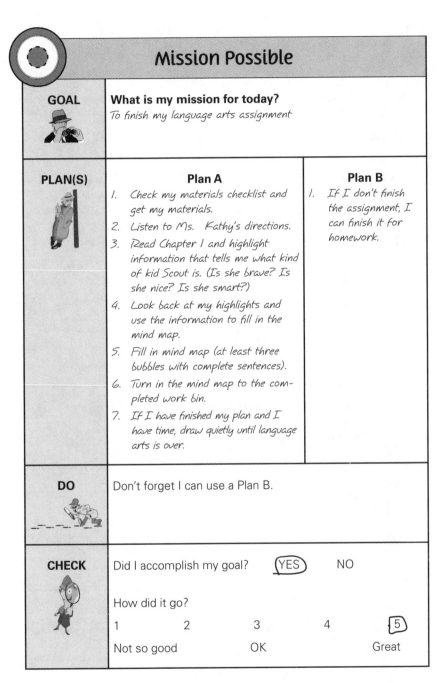

GOAL	**What is my mission for today?** To finish my language arts assignment

PLAN(S)

Plan A

1. Check my materials checklist and get my materials.
2. Listen to Ms. Kathy's directions.
3. Read Chapter 1 and highlight information that tells me what kind of kid Scout is. (Is she brave? Is she nice? Is she smart?)
4. Look back at my highlights and use the information to fill in the mind map.
5. Fill in mind map (at least three bubbles with complete sentences).
6. Turn in the mind map to the completed work bin.
7. If I have finished my plan and I have time, draw quietly until language arts is over.

Plan B

1. If I don't finish the assignment, I can finish it for homework.

DO

Don't forget I can use a Plan B.

CHECK

Did I accomplish my goal?   (YES)   NO

How did it go?

1   2   3   4   5

Not so good   OK   Great

Mission Possible

GOAL	**What is my mission for today?** *To finish my math assignment*

PLAN(S)	**Plan A** 1. Mad Minute 2. Complete word problem. 3. Complete problems 20 to 30. Remember that to earn the points, I need to show my work. 4. Turn completed work into the completed work bin. 5. If I have finished the plan and I have time, I can draw quietly until math is over.	**Plan B** 1. If I don't finish the assignment, I can finish it for homework.

DO	Don't forget I can use a Plan B.

CHECK	Did I accomplish my goal? (YES) NO How did it go? 1 2 3 {4} 5 Not so good OK Great

Appendix

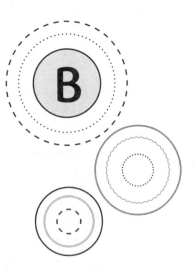

*Sample Individualized
Education Program Goals
and Accommodations that
Address Executive Dysfunction*

GENERAL BEST PRACTICE PRINCIPLES WHEN WRITING EXECUTIVE FUNCTION INDIVIDUALIZED EDUCATION PROGRAM GOALS

- The purpose of the goals should be that the child learns to use self-regulatory routines and scripts (or habits) that increase independent, flexible, goal-oriented problem solving at school (this includes the classroom, lunchroom, bathroom, playground, and other relevant settings).

- EF goals cannot be successfully met unless they are introduced with a lot of individualized structuring, cueing, and reinforcement. Simply showing a child with executive dysfunction how to fill out an agenda book will not enable that child to do so independently on a regular basis. Intensive practice with an adult, followed by the implementation of key cues such as a written checklist, and the slow fading of direct adult support as the child becomes more independent, is required.

- It is essential to establish the necessary external environmental preconditions (e.g., a "safe address" at school, visual cues) that facilitate and promote the child's developing and making automatic (if possible) self-regulatory routines and scripts.

- Because executive dysfunction affects all aspects of school performance, IEP goals should link directly to all key academic content areas (e.g., reading, writing, math, science) as well as to communication and socioemotional performance.

- Use the sample IEP goals that follow as starting points or models for specific IEP goals.

- There are three key areas in an IEP in which a child's EF can be addressed: Present Levels of Academic Achievement and Functional Performance (where the team can list a child's areas of strength and needs), Goals, and Accommodations and Modifications (where the team can list a child's needs for supports (e.g., provide visuals, use written recipes and routines).

- Work with your team to try to establish how much progress to anticipate in the coming year, and make sure that achievement of goals is measured throughout the year with criterion-based instruments wherever possible.

SAMPLE GOALS

The following sample goals were written for an imaginary child named Sam.

1. Flexible problem solving

   a. Given training in, and visual reminders of, self-regulatory scripts (e.g., "big deal/little deal," "choice/no choice," "plan A/plan B," and "handling the unexpected"), Sam will manage unexpected events and violations of routine without disrupting classroom activities.

   b. With fading adult supports, Sam will use a structured recipe or routine for generating new ideas, or brainstorming, to respond successfully to open-ended assignments.

   c. When faced with changes and/or transitions in activities or environments, Sam will initiate the new activity after only two (or one, or three) reminders (or within 2, 4, 5 minutes).

   d. Given concrete training, visual supports, and fading adult cuing, Sam will correctly label flexible and stuck behaviors in himself.

   e. Given training, practice, visual supports, and fading adult cuing in the use of specific coping strategies, Sam will identify and use a coping strategy when he indicates that he is stuck or upset.

f. Given training and practice with the concept of compromise, and in the presence of visual supports, Sam will accept and generate compromise solutions to conflicts when working cooperatively with others.

2. Goal setting

a. Sam will participate with teachers and therapists in setting instructional and therapy goals (e.g., I want to be able to read this book, hit a baseball into the outfield, write a story so Mom can read it)

b. Given explicit instruction, visual reminders, and fading adult support, Sam will successfully distinguish target goals (e.g., doing well in school, making a friend, learning to read, graduating from school) from whims or off-target behavior (e.g., playing video games instead of doing homework).

3. Planning

a. Given a routine (e.g., complete a sheet of math problems, ask a friend to play a game), Sam will indicate what steps or items are needed and the order of the events.

b. Sam will learn a general self-regulatory script (e.g., Goal, Plan, Do, Check) for carrying out any multiple-step task (e.g., completing homework, writing an essay, doing a science project) and—given practice, visual cues, and fading adult supports—will apply the script independently to new situations.

c. Given a selection of three activities for a therapy or instructional session, Sam will indicate their order, create a plan on paper, and stick to the plan.

d. Given a task that he correctly identifies as difficult for him, Sam will create a plan for accomplishing the task.

e. If he fails to achieve a predicted grade on a test, Sam will create a plan for improving performance for the next test.

4. Organizing

   a. Given adult support and visual cues, Sam will create a system for organizing personal items in his cubby.

   b. To tell an organized story, Sam will place photographs in order and then narrate the sequence of events.

   c. Given visual cues and fading adult support, Sam will select and use a system to organize his assignments and other schoolwork.

   d. Given a complex task, Sam will organize the task on paper, including the materials needed, the steps to accomplish the task, and a time frame.

   e. Using learned strategies and given fading adult support, Sam will prepare an organized outline before proceeding with writing projects.

5. Self-monitoring, self-evaluating

   a. Given training in a self-regulatory routine, such as Goal, Plan, Do, Check, and visual cues and fading adult supports, Sam will accurately predict how effectively he will accomplish a task. For example, he will accurately predict whether he will be able to complete a task, predict how many (of something) he can finish, predict his grade on tests, predict how many problems he will be able to complete in a specific time period.

   b. Given a specific work-checking routine, Sam will identify errors in his work without teacher assistance.

   c. Sam's rating of his performance on a 10-point scale will be within one point of the teacher's rating.

6. Self-awareness and self-advocacy

   a. Given a specific routine for monitoring task success, such as Goal, Plan, Do, Check, Sam will accurately identify tasks that are easy or difficult for him.

   b. Given a difficult task, Sam will (verbally or nonverbally) indicate that it is difficult.

c. Sam will explain why some tasks are easy or difficult for him.

d. Sam will request help when tasks are difficult.

e. Sam will offer help to others when he is more capable than the other child.

SAMPLE ACCOMMODATIONS FOR SAM

1. *Free access to a safe address:* Give Sam passes that allow him access to a trusted adult at school (e.g., counselor, special education teacher, or other person who is there every day) when he is becoming overloaded or confused.

2. *Preferential seating:* Seat Sam close to teachers and away from distractions. Provide quiet, isolated study areas, such as a cubicle, for independent assignments.

3. *Minimize and preview transitions.* Preview upcoming changes (e.g., predict teacher absence or field trip, tour new classroom, meet new teacher). Structure Sam's schedule to have the fewest possible transitions during the day.

4. *Post schedules and routines* in the classroom.

5. *Teach Sam in a step-by-step fashion.* Break complex activities into simple step-by-step tasks. Give Sam recipes, written routines, and checklists for multiple-step tasks (e.g., long division, packing up to go home, writing a paragraph). Provide visual and graphic organizers.

6. *Develop standard operating procedures (SOPs) for all jobs or tasks.* SOPs should be clear, step-by-step instructions for how to carry out a specific task. The SOP should be completed and include all steps, even if they appear obvious, because it only takes one missing step to derail an activity. Included in the task analysis should be a list of all materials that are needed to complete the task and all information for the task. Keep these in a single notebook clearly labeled "Standard Operating Procedures Manual." Pages should be numbered, and there should be a table of contents indicating which SOPs are on which pages for quick reference.

7. *Support organizational deficits.* Sam is often highly capable of completing appropriately modified or adapted assignments. However, in many situations, he does not know how to get started, loses or misplaces work, or gets overwhelmed by the details. Set up his classroom and structure coursework to accommodate these areas of need:

   a. Review homework assignments with him before he leaves school to ensure that he has the assignment clearly recorded, has the appropriate materials, and can do a sample problem. It may be best for Sam to write out the specific rules or plan for completing the homework at the top of the pages that will be used for homework.

   b. Indicate how long Sam should spend on specific assignments. Use a timer for work sessions to reduce the open-ended nature of the work.

   c. Organize Sam's work area so that everything is readily available, identifiable, and uncluttered. This may require a weekly desk clean-out or check.

   d. Make use of e-mail or other mechanisms for frequent contact between home and school, so that Sam's parents are aware of any missing assignments or special requirements. Assist with the maintenance and organization of a notebook that contains color-coded labels, a table of contents, and clearly labeled pockets for school assignments and important communications between home and school.

8. *Reduce visual stimulation in classroom.* Seat Sam facing the least cluttered wall or space in the room.

9. *Use appropriate aids* in the classroom, such as a calculator to check work, graph paper to help keep work organized, and a special box to hold assignments. Allow Sam to use a computer to learn about new topics, complete individually paced academic curricula, and produce work in multiple modalities, including PowerPoint presentations.

10. *Keep oral directions brief, or accompany them with a visual reminder* such as a checklist.

11. *Limit handwriting requirements.* Provide class notes (copies of a good notetaker's notes or teacher outlines) to minimize note-taking. Make word processing equipment fully available to Sam for written assignments. Standard keyboarding position should not be required when Sam types. Take dictation.

12. *Make accommodations regarding the quantity of home and class work* Sam completes, and provide extended time for in-class assignments. Limit homework and classwork expectations to the number of problems Sam can complete in a given time period. If the teacher wishes Sam to spend 30 minutes on a writing assignment, assign an amount of work that can be completed in that time.

13. *Apply testing accommodations, including extended time.* Allow Sam additional time to complete tests. Also consider allowing Sam to demonstrate knowledge in a variety of ways; for example, by answering short-answer questions or fill-in-the-blank rather than essays, or by allowing him to respond to open-ended questions using bulleted lists rather than lengthy narratives.

14. *Provide Sam with scheduled and spontaneous downtime.* Sam's struggle to maintain appropriate social behavior and to understand the social interactions in the classroom cannot be underestimated. Sam is in essence "trapped" for most of the day in a very challenging situation that requires extra effort simply to comply with basic social conventions in the classroom. A break away from this may reduce the level of stress and anxiety he experiences and improve behavior.

15. *Allow Sam to eat lunch in a small, quiet group.*

16. *Teach new or difficult skills using topics of special interest to Sam.* When tackling writing skills, for example, let Sam write about his favorite topic.

17. *Individualized teacher selection:* Children like Sam are extremely sensitive to their teachers and require unusually skilled individuals who have both excellent organizational skills and provide a highly structured, routine-based classroom and are also warm and flexible in their interpersonal interactions with children.

18. *Curriculum flexibility:* Sam will benefit from opportunities to accelerate his learning and to work at an independent pace when possible. In general, weighting his or her curriculum toward computers and subjects that are amenable to gathering information through reading and visual presentation is strongly encouraged.

19. *Explicit emphasis on self-esteem:* Provide concrete charts of progress and verbal reinforcement. Segment assignments in small, manageable pieces, and identify opportunities in the curriculum to allow Sam to express particular areas of expertise. Many children such as Sam gain great pleasure from teaching others, and opportunities for him to present materials to the class should be carefully considered. This is more generally associated with flexible curriculum development that encourages Sam to develop areas of interest with projects.

Index

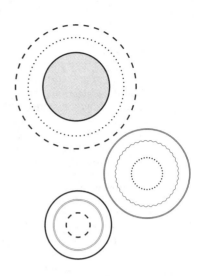

Page numbers followed by *f* and *t* indicate figures and tables, respectively.

- -

- -

Responsibility chart, 73f
Restaurants, modeling flexibility, 34
Rewards
    case studies, 72–73, 73–75, 73f, 75f
    for coping strategies, 109–110
    examples, 82, 86, 87f
    importance of, 81–82
    for parents and family members, 103
    for staying on target, 67–68
    tangible reminders, 86
Routines
    breaking down into steps, 93, 97–99
    disruptions in, preparing for, 90
    establishing, 89
    importance of, 88–89
    for multistep tasks, 97–98
    sample accommodations, 153
    sample individualized education
        program (IEP) goals, 150–151
    sample morning checklist, 100f
Rules, for multistep tasks, 97–98

"Safe addresses"
    identifying, 117–118
    sample individualized education
        program (IEP) accommodation,
        153
School
    curriculum goals, 17, 156
    overload, avoiding feelings of, 92–93
    vignettes, 10t–12t
    see also Classroom activities; Indi-
        vidualized education program
        (IEP)
School notebook, creating, sample
    worksheet, 143–144
Science assignment, case study exam-
    ple, 75–76
Screen time
    controlling, 126
    see also Technology use
Scripts, see Key words and scripts
Self-advocacy/self-awareness
    encouraging, 118
    sample individualized education
        program (IEP) goals, 152–153
Self-esteem
    goal setting and, 43
    sample accommodations for
        enhancing, 156

Self-monitoring
    as aspect of executive function (EF),
        6
    individualized education program
        (IEP) goals, 149, 151, 152
    self-soothing routines, 88–89
    technology supports for, 125
Self-talk, versus visual supports, 100
Sensory sensitivities
    characteristics of children with
        autism spectrum disorder
        (ASD), 120
    strategies for, 91–92
Sharing, teaching about, 50
Shopping
    flexibility, modeling, 37
    Goal, Plan, Do, Check (GPDC)
        approach, 47
    staying on target, modeling, 66
Smell, sense of, 91
Soccer participation, sample work-
    sheet, 138
Social interactions
    characteristics of children with
        autism spectrum disorder
        (ASD), 119
    providing breaks from, 14–15, 91
    technology supports for, 123
Social networks
    fostering social interactions, 123
    parental support, 104–105
Socratic method, 80, 118
Software, see Technology use
SOPs, see Standard operating proce-
    dures (SOPs), developing
Space, for retreating from overstimu-
    lation, 92
Spelling, technology supports for, 125
Sports participation, sample work-
    sheet, 138
Standard operating procedures
    (SOPs), developing, 153
Stores, see Shopping
Strengths
    building on, 80
    of children with autism spectrum
        disorder (ASD), 80
    inherited nature of, 106
    knowledge base of children with
        autism spectrum disorder
        (ASD), 12–13